Exploring Religious Conflict

Gregory F. Treverton, Heather S. Gregg,
Daniel Gibran, Charles W. Yost

RAND NATIONAL SECURITY RESEARCH DIVISION

The proceedings described in this report were hosted by the RAND National Security Research Division, which conducts research and analysis for the Office of the Secretary of Defense, the Joint Staff, the Unified Commands, the defense agencies, the Department of the Navy, the U.S. intelligence community, allied foreign governments, and foundations.

ISBN: 0-8330-3804-4

The RAND Corporation is a nonprofit research organization providing objective analysis and effective solutions that address the challenges facing the public and private sectors around the world. RAND's publications do not necessarily reflect the opinions of its research clients and sponsors.

RAND® is a registered trademark.

Published 2005 by the RAND Corporation
1776 Main Street, P.O. Box 2138, Santa Monica, CA 90407-2138
1200 South Hayes Street, Arlington, VA 22202-5050
201 North Craig Street, Suite 202, Pittsburgh, PA 15213-1516
RAND URL: http://www.rand.org/
To order RAND documents or to obtain additional information, contact
Distribution Services: Telephone: (310) 451-7002;
Fax: (310) 451-6915; Email: order@rand.org

PREFACE

It has been said that the United States is "India governed by Sweden" — that is, a religious country with a very secular tradition of government. Thus, it is perhaps little surprise that government, more than society, finds it awkward to address religious motivations, especially for violence. Yet September 11th drove home that the nation, and its intelligence, can no longer fail to address such issues directly. To that end, the RAND Corporation organized a board of religious experts. Those experts met with intelligence analysts in three carefully prepared day-long workshops.

The goal was to provide analysts with background and frames of reference by assessing religious motivations in international politics, what may cause violence with religious roots and how states have sought to take advantage of or contain religious violence. This report summarizes and extends those workshops. The project was funded by the CIA's Directorate of Intelligence, but neither the task force's analyses nor the contents of this report are based on intelligence reporting. The report thus does not represent official views but, rather, those of the task force participants. In addition to analysts, it should be of interest to policy-makers and to interested citizens who find killing in the name of religion all but unfathomable.

We especially express our appreciation to the experts — Mark Juergensmeyer, Philip Jenkins, Juan Cole, Ian Lustick and Jack Miles. This research was conducted within the Intelligence Policy Center (IPC) of the RAND National Security Research Division (NSRD). NSRD conducts research and analysis for the Office of the Secretary of Defense, the Joint Staff, the Unified Commands, the defense agencies, the Department

of the Navy, the U.S. intelligence community, allied foreign
governments, and foundations.

Comments are more than welcome. The principal author can be reached
by email at Greg_Treverton@rand.org. The director of the RAND
Intelligence Policy Center is John Parachini. For more information about
the Center, please contact him by email, John_Parachini@rand.org, or by
phone at 703-413-1100, extension 5579. More information about RAND is
available at www.rand.org.

CONTENTS

FIGURES

TABLES

SUMMARY

After September 11th, it almost goes without saying that religious violence in the name of a holy cause has escalated. Killing in the name of God constitutes a major driver of violent conflicts today. No major religion has been, or is today, a stranger to violence from its extremists, and that violence will pose challenges for U.S. foreign policy and for the analysts who seek to inform that policy. So, too, comparisons across forms of religious violence are instructive. New Religious Movements (NRMs) — which are almost always offshoots, however bizarre, of major religious traditions — have also emerged as sources of violence. Yet Islamic extremists are now in a class by themselves as a threat to the United States, as a transnational, non-state movement with the chance to appeal to a billion and a half people. Understanding these phenomena, Islamic extremism in particular, and their implications for policymaking and the intelligence community are major aims of this report. It is divided into three sections — "cosmic war," states and religiously motivated violence, and New Religious Movements.

COSMIC WAR AND ITS SOURCES

Mark Juergensmeyer's concept of "cosmic war" provides a useful conceptual framework for examining the larger-than-life confrontations that religious extremists are engaged in today. This concept refers to the metaphysical battle between the forces of Good and Evil that enlivens the religious imagination and compels violent action.

Cosmic war has roots in the theology of most religions. In the three monotheistic religions, it is the Day of Judgment, the cosmic battle between Good and Evil, and the realization of God's ultimate purpose for His creation. In Hinduism and Buddhism, it is the perennial struggle to exit the Wheel of Existences with its continuous cycle of rebirths in order to return to Brahman or achieve Nirvana. Cosmic war ensues when this inner conflict between Good and Evil becomes manifest — physical, not metaphysical.

Cosmic war has several defining characteristics: It is more symbolic than pragmatic in intent and is performed in remarkably dramatic ways; its displays of violence find their moral justification in a religious imperative; it operates on a divine time line with victory being imminent but not in this lifetime; and it is empowering to those who take up the cause, providing divinely justified actions to real-world problems.

Finally, acts of terror in a cosmic war are seen as evocations of a larger spiritual confrontation between Good and Evil. The power of this concept surpasses all ordinary claims of political and earthly authority. In the Middle East and other parts of the Muslim world where the battle for the soul of Islam continues, Islamists and Al-Qaeda's networks have placed their struggle against secularism, perceived Western domination, and the United States, in a cosmic context. This context animates and elevates their struggle giving it the imprimatur of the divine; hence the outcome of their fight is preordained: Islam in its pristine purity will prevail.

STATES AND RELIGIOUSLY MOTIVATED VIOLENCE

States have tended to approach religious opposition tactically rather than strategically. Countries such as Saudi Arabia and Pakistan have focused on short-term political gains using the most expedient tools available to counter religious opposition — from concessions on social issues to crackdowns on political opposition. The history of changing and shortsighted state policies toward religious opposition suggests these approaches are not sustainable in the long term. Nor have states shown much success in managing the spiritual/ideological dimension of conflict once it has begun — even if they started to stir religious passions in the first place.

Political "wars of position," a concept coined by the Italian socialist Antonio Gramsci, is useful in understanding the types of states that use religion for political gain and in what ways they accomplish it. "Cosmic war," may be initiated by an extremist vanguard, but that may only be the first phase of the struggle. The next phase of conflict might be termed a "war of positioning," in which various actors with competing agendas jockey for greater influence in and control over the state.

It is also important to offer a careful definition of radical political "fundamentalism" as distinct from radical apolitical fundamentalism, on the one hand, and from areligious political radicalism, on the other. For starters, radical fundamentalists might be defined as those who fit three criteria:

- They call for a radical, rapid, and comprehensive transformation of society.
- They believe that there is some direct link between adherents and the ultimate source of authority in the cosmos.
- They engage in politics to achieve their purposes.

Table 1 locates fundamentalism by comparison to categories based on different answers to the three criteria.

Table 1

Fundamentalists Compared to Others

	Radical	Direct	Politics
Fundamentalists	Yes	Yes	Yes
Pietists, quietists	Yes	Yes	No
Utopian pragmatists, socialists	Yes	No	Yes
Fascist parties in fascist states	No	Yes	Yes
Yippies	Yes	No	No
Parties in pluralist democracies	No	No	Yes
Transcendental meditators	No	Yes	No
"Kiwanis Club"	No	No	No

In particular, the Iran case under Ayatollah Khomeini offers insights into the "fundamentalist" phenomenon because it demonstrates how a "quietist" posture was transformed into politico-fundamentalist fervor. And it presents a dramatic example of this fusion between religion and politics in the 20th century. Political rule by clerics was a Khomeini-inspired innovation in Shiism. His message combined religion, politics, and nationalism, and his call for political action was not only appealing to the masses but it galvanized them into taking action against the Shah.

The Khomeini experiment in Iran was a watershed event. It emboldened Muslims across the world, making them more politically active and inspiring their fundamentalist fervor, and ultimately leading to radicalization of new groups such as the Mahdi Army under Muqtada al-Sadr in Iraq.

NEW RELIGIOUS MOVEMENTS (NRMs)

Sometimes referred to as cults, NRMs have two defining characteristics — a high degree of tension between the group and its surrounding society and a high degree of control exercised by leaders over their members. There is a discernible proliferation of NRMs across the global landscape. While they have gotten most attention in the richer countries, they are found everywhere, including countries of the Third World and the Middle East. Nor are NRMs unique to one religious tradition. NRMs can be found in Hinduism (the Rashtriya Swayamsevak Sangh, or RSS), Israel (Gush Emunim), Christianity (the U.S.-based Identity Movement) and Islam, including Al Qaeda, a global network with a transcendent vision that draws support in the defense of Islam. While most are not violent, a few have engaged in ritualized acts of mass suicide and homicide. Notable examples include Heaven's Gate, the Branch Davidians, and Aum Shinrikyo.

Among possible conditions under which NRMs resort to violence, two stand out — if the group or movement feels threatened from the outside, by society or the government; and if it has young, inexperienced leaders that resort to violence when threatened either from inside or outside the movement. Therefore, a government's policies with regard to an NRM, if perceived as threatening, could prompt the group to resort to violence.

The Sadr movement in Iraq fits the definition of a NRM in many respects; it is a minority within the Shia population and is marked by a high degree of control and allegiance from those surrounding Muqtada. He and his movement became symbols of resistance to the U.S.-led coalition forces and to more politically quietist Shia leaders in Iraq, such as the Grand Ayatollah al-Sistani, who neither overtly challenged the occupation nor called for the creation of a Shia-dominated Islamic state.

POLICY AND INTELLIGENCE IMPLICATIONS

For the intelligence analyst and for policymaking, an understanding of cosmic war is particularly useful when formulating strategies aimed at its mitigation. In particular, the use of military force as a tool for combating cosmic war could be counterproductive; force could perpetuate the perception that a religious group is under attack and must fight for the preservation of the faith and its own existence. It validates the appeal of cosmic war.

Intelligence analysis should pay close attention to religious language, to its style and substance, its historical context and symbolic content, and its deeper meanings and cultural undertones. Religious language could provide clues to determine whether and when groups see their battles as cosmic. Intelligence analysis should also look for identifiable state actions that trigger the perception of a cosmic war in progress.

Examples of such action might include coalition forces' decision to arrest Muqtada al-Sadr and forcibly disarm his movement in Iraq, as well as U.S. government policy in the Israeli-Palestinian conflict that risks looking completely one-sided to the Muslim world. More generally, in dealing with a perceived clash between Islam and current U.S. foreign policy, an attempt ought to be made to blur the edges of that clash, not sharpen them. Instead of emphasizing the historic sense of conflict between Islam and Christianity or the West, policy ought to emphasize possible points of convergence.

ACRONYMS

Symbol	Definition
CIA	Central Intelligence Agency
FBI	Federal Bureau of Investigation
NRM	New Religious Movement
OTI	Office of Transnational Issues
RSS	Rashtriya Swayamsevak Sangh
SCIRI	Supreme Council for Islamic Revolution in Iraq
ZOG	Zionist Occupation Government

1. INTRODUCTION

The numbers support what September 11th indicated so graphically:
Religious conflicts have escalated dramatically since the onset of the
Cold War. According to one scholar's estimates, throughout the 1950-1996
period, religious conflicts constituted between 33 and 47 percent of all
conflicts.[1] Moreover, since the end of the Cold War, nonreligious
conflicts have decreased more than religious conflicts.[2] Increasingly,
religion is both an identifiable source of violence around the world and
simultaneously so deeply interwoven into other sources of violence —
including economic, ideological, territorial, and ethnic sources — that
it is difficult to isolate. While certainly not a new phenomenon,
religiously motivated violence has become a pervasive element of modern
conflicts. "Holy terror," killing in the name of God, constitutes a
major driver of violent conflicts today. This is evident in the rise of
Islamic insurgencies in places like Chechnya and Afghanistan and in
terrorist attacks in Saudi Arabia and Indonesia as well as in the West,
including Spain and the United States.

To be sure, the rationale for religiously motivated violence exists
in Judaism, Christianity, Hinduism, and elsewhere. No major religious
tradition has been or is a stranger to violence from its extremists.
Some of that violence will challenge American foreign policy, and all of
it will challenge the understanding of the U.S. intelligence analysts.

That said, while the focus on militant Islam is marked and
unsurprising after September 11th, it is also appropriate, because
Islamic extremism is in a class by itself as a threat to the United
States. It is an international, non-state movement with the opportunity
to appeal to a billion and a half adherents. In that sense, it is
without parallel in the contemporary world. It constitutes a one-member
set. No movement with its origins in Christianity, Judaism, Hinduism, or
any other religion has disrupted international security to the extent
that this movement has done and will continue to do.

However, while the focus needs to remain on Islamist terrorism, it
is nonetheless illuminating to consider the psychology of Islamist

terrorism in comparative context. The psychology of "cosmic war" is instructive across major religious borders. This psychology rewards comparative consideration. Similarly, while the roots of Islamic terror run deep in history, Islamist terrorism in important regards is a new development within world Islam and deserves comparative consideration alongside other new religious movements. Under what identifiable circumstances do these movements sometimes develop homicidal or suicidal tendencies?

For example, when religious extremists are convinced that their cause is sacred and ordained by God, they are capable of savage and relentless violence. And what is striking about "religious terrorism" is that "it is almost exclusively symbolic, performed in remarkably dramatic ways."[3] This is not to say, of course, that this violence is not real but only that it is meaningful to its perpetrators in ways that defy entirely pragmatic explanation.

This report offers an introductory inquiry into the causes and motivations of religiously inspired violence and terrorism. It is distilled from a series of workshops on religious conflict sponsored by the CIA's Directorate of Intelligence and the RAND Corporation. The goal of the project was to explore religiously motivated conflict in the presence of some of the best experts inside and outside of government.

The report is divided into five sections. After this introduction, Section 2 uses the concept of sociologist Mark Juergensmeyer's "cosmic war" as an entry point for examining some of the motivations of religiously inspired violence. Section 3 examines the role that states play in exacerbating religious violence and looks at possible avenues of mitigating the rise of religious bellicosity. Section 4 evaluates New Religious Movements (NRMs) and explores the conditions under which NRMs become violent. And Section 5 offers concluding remarks and the report's implications for policies aimed at mitigating religious violence.

2. ASSESSING THE THREAT OF "COSMIC" WAR

Sociologist Mark Juergensmeyer[4] coined the phrase "cosmic war" to describe the worldview of religious adherents who have resorted to violence in defense of their faith. Specifically, Juergensmeyer defines cosmic war as "larger than life" confrontations in which divine battles between Good and Evil, commonly portrayed in the scriptures of most religions, are believed to be occurring in the here-and-now. Thus "cosmic war" refers to the metaphysical battle between Good and Evil that enlivens the religious imagination. Through symbol, myth, and ritual, religion proclaims the primacy of order over chaos in the universe or cosmos, and the ultimate victory of Good over Evil is won by cosmic war. For example, in Christianity, cosmic war is understood to mean the "great controversy" between Christ and Satan, between the forces of "good" and "evil" for the salvation of humankind.

Juergensmeyer identifies several characteristics of cosmic war, including the demonization of the enemy, the promise of divine rewards for earthly sacrifice, and the belief that the war cannot be lost but, at the same time, is unwinnable in this lifetime. Believers who demonize their enemy and justify the killing of "noncombatants" tend to do so by drawing sharp lines between the two worlds of the spiritual and the temporal, between the metaphysical and the mundane. Acts of terror are conceived as evocations of a larger spiritual confrontation, and immediate victory may not be the expectation or even the goal of such acts. The acts of violence unleashed by these believers are construed as symbolic, designed to make a statement rather than actually disable the enemy, which is often a secular state. Confrontations are likely to be characterized as cosmic war, according to Juergensmeyer, when the political struggle is perceived as a defense of basic identity and dignity, when losing the struggle would be unthinkable, and when the struggle cannot be won in real time or in real terms.

EXAMINING THE SOURCES OF RELIGIOUSLY MOTIVATED VIOLENCE

Juergensmeyer argues that all religious traditions feature depictions of divine wars in which Good battles Evil, particularly in a religion's scriptures. Divine conflicts are featured prominently in the apocalyptic theology of the three monotheistic religions, Judaism, Christianity, and Islam. In Judaism, it is the final judgment and the realization of God's purpose for creation. In Islam, it is the spiritual Jihad, the struggle in a believer's life to overcome evil and to do good, to live according to Allah's will and defend the community of believers against all infidels. And in Hinduism, a pantheistic religion, it was not merely confined to the fierce physical struggles between Lord Rama and Rawana, the Evil One, but also included a struggle that linked the battlefield of Ayodhya to the daily lives of all Hindus. To investigate this claim of cosmic or divine war, Juergensmeyer interviewed members of religious groups ranging from Aum Shinrikyo to Hamas to the Christian Identity movement in the United States.

In all these movements, he found strong echoes of cosmic war. This philosophy provides a cosmic battlefield where forces for Good are called to fight some unspeakable Evil. These warrior believers fight for a holy cause, and all actions are taken in the name of God and justified. Moreover, cosmic war provides the "template of meaning" for these individuals and groups. Not only does it explain why things are as they are, but it also provides the foundation for doing something, for taking action. In other words, cosmic war bridges the spiritual world and real world. It provides a way to link individual cognition and the real world to divine notions of Good versus Evil. Cosmic war links real and often personal issues and problems to a broader community and shared worldview of great struggle in the spiritual and temporal world. Then it links this worldview back to real actions that individuals can perform, which also has symbolic meaning in the spiritual world.

Juergensmeyer further argues that terrorist acts stemming from cosmic war are not strategic in the sense that they aim to accomplish concrete purposes. Rather, they are symbolic, intended to demonstrate to the terrorists' supporters and potential supporters the reality of a war that the rest of the world neither sees nor comprehends. Juergensmeyer

illustrates this point by describing an interview with Mahmud
Abouhalima, one of the principal perpetrators in the World Trade Center
attacks in 1993. When questioned about the attacks, Abouhalima
responded: "There is a war going on and you don't realize it. It is the
battle of Truth and Evil. After Oklahoma City, you knew it. Terrorism,
even 9-11, is aimed as much at potential supporters as at us. It is for
the watchers of Al Jazeera." And when the World Trade Center towers came
down on September 11th, the perpetrators and al-Qaeda understood this as
metaphor, "as choice signifiers of the confrontation between absolute
good threatened with destruction by its absolute opposite."[5] This
dualistic, Manichean struggle between right and wrong, between the
forces of Good and Evil, calls the chosen into a holy war with drastic
consequences. If the holy warrior loses, God's creation is lost and
chaos and evil will prevail.

The cosmic context animates war in several distinct ways. First, it
not only links the divine with the temporal, it is also an exciting and
ennobling venture in the cause of God. It provides the conceptual lens
through which the cosmic battle between Good and Evil are perceived, and
the ultimate justification for engaging in acts of violence. Moreover,
cosmic war is long-term; it is God's war, and in the long run God never
loses. Even if the battle today is not won, the overall war will succeed
and Good will eventually prevail over Evil. This is God's design and it
cannot fail. Moreover, cosmic warriors cannot accept the world as it is.
Even though they know that they will kill innocent people by engaging in
violence, they willingly accept this burden because of their compelling
desire to do God's will, to do what He commands. They justify violence
by convincing themselves that the rampant evil in, and injustices of,
society far outweigh the amount of harm caused by their actions. In
other words, violence becomes necessary to save society from cosmic
evil.

Juergensmeyer further contends that cosmic war requires demonizing
or satanizing the enemy. The enemy is not merely humans fighting for
material gains but cosmic foes bent on the destruction of Good. This
satanization process, while ultimately creating a larger-than-life
enemy, does not occur in a complete vacuum; it usually has its roots in

the enemy's policies and actions. Al-Qaeda, for example, and bin-Laden in particular, has taken the American military presence in Saudi Arabia, which many Muslims oppose, and translated it into an event with cosmic implications. In other words, he sees America's occupation of Islam's holy places as a diabolical act by an infidel power that should therefore be fiercely resisted.

Crucially, Juergensmeyer stresses that cosmic war is always defensive. However, unlike other aspects or forms of defensive warfare, the "defensive" element of cosmic war is predicated on two necessary conditions, "imminence" and "human agency."[6] The warriors in God's army must believe that the day of deliverance is near — imminent. And they must also think that their human action would lead or usher in the messianic era. For example, a believer who embraces the imminence of the messianic era thinks that he can "force the end" by resorting to violence. Cosmic war is also a response to victimization. For the believers, cosmic war can be empowering and the rewards intimate and personal. Moreover, rewards are not measured in earthly terms, but in divine promises of salvation and paradise. In Islam, for example, the personal benefits that await the warrior who was martyred in God's holy war transcend anything earthly. These benefits, found in *hadiths*, sayings of the Prophet Muhammad, are said to include the forgiving of the martyr's sins, the redemption from the torments of the grave, security from the fear of hell, a crown of glory featuring a ruby of inestimable worth, marriage to 72 huris, or black-eyed virgins, and the ability to extend these heavenly privileges to 70 relatives.[7]

Policies aimed at "undoing" cosmic war are difficult, precisely because responses to cosmic war, especially the use of military force, can so easily be turned to validate the claims of the cosmic warriors. For that reason, Juergensmeyer is skeptical of military responses. The more the conflict is militarized, the more the warriors will be validated in the righteousness of their own cause or struggle and in the eyes of all onlookers, and the more the United States will become the evil enemy. Indeed, as others point out, even the language of a "global war on terrorism" plays into Islamic jihadists' hands, as does the notion that "if you're not with us, you're against us." Al-Qaeda's religious extremists may pay careful attention to the language used by members of the U.S. Administration. They may listen not only for style and content but also for concepts that demonize them and their cause. These images play into the language and worldview of cosmic war.

Moreover, it is worth noting that the visions of cosmic war, however seemingly fantastic and farfetched, may appear to be imminent. September 11th did draw the United States into a protracted war, drive it deeper into debt, and weaken its standing among the world's Muslims. By these measures, it was a success.

Other cases suggest that a limited and localized response can help keep cosmic war from spreading. One example of such an approach is India's battles with Sikh political separatists and religious extremism. India has succeeded in containing the violence within one region, the Punjab. While the conflict in Northern Ireland was primarily political, the British government managed a proportional response, focusing instead on negotiating and not responding to terrorist acts from fringe groups. Over time, Britain has been able to "de-satanize" itself (as it also de-satanized its enemy). Inaction or doing nothing can be difficult though, particularly because of pressures from domestic constituencies to respond forcibly.

Juergensmeyer notes, however, that cosmic war sometimes collapses from within, from schisms or from the warriors scaring themselves or would-be supporters. An example of this is the Oklahoma City terrorist attack on the Alfred P. Murrah Federal Office Building in April 1995. While Timothy McVeigh saw himself as a fundamentalist Christian and regarded himself as acting in defense of the faith, he ended up horrifying the people he intended to defend and they turned against him and his actions. McVeigh was a member of a violent Christian white supremacist group that is millenarian in outlook. Most, if not all, of these groups, such as the American Christian Patriot movement and Christian Identity, orient their members toward violence by appeals to arcane theological interpretations of scripture. And herein lies the cosmic dimension of their struggle.

Cosmic war, therefore, has psychological and socio-psychological roots. Much attention has been paid to the supposed psychological underpinnings and profiles of the 9-11 hijackers. Available evidence suggests that most of them came from backgrounds of relative comfort and were educated and savvy about the foreign environments in which they lived. Muhammad Atta, the leader, for example, was an urban planning specialist by training and came from a well-to-do Egyptian family. Almost all of them had higher university degrees, and all of them had a fervent dislike for the United States. However, these observations miss why some individuals who may be considered "failures" by Western standards become cosmic warriors and others do not. Moreover, it cannot be the case that all the Al-Qaeda recruits were failures.

Thus, the interesting questions are not psychological but socio-psychological. What animates them to act, to take up arms and kill indiscriminately? This question suggests that causation might run in the opposite direction: Once individuals are known to have become radicalized, they are shunned in their own societies, such that participation in these movements can itself transform people into failures. But on the other hand, participation in some contexts is considered brave and heroic. The Palestinian struggle against Israel, for example, is a case in point where individual warriors, volunteers for martyrdom, are given the highest honor. This is particularly so in a culture that extols dignity and honor. Thus, a *shaheed* (witness, martyr) who dies in Allah's war against the enemy reaches a kind of transcendent fame in his community.

It may be worth distinguishing those "corrigible" groups, like Hamas, who have achievable goals, from the "incorrigible" ones like Aum Shinrikyo, which are millenarian - seeking Armageddon, not independence or a change in governmental policy. Yet when Juergensmeyer talked to Dr. Abdul Aziz Rantisi of Hamas, Rantisi was at pains to stress that Hamas was not about territorial liberation but spiritual liberation, not about an ephemeral struggle with a definite timeframe but about a cosmic one that transcends time; it was about honor and Islam, not just a state.

Finally, does cosmic war require religious faith, or can atheists or lapsed deists be drawn into a cosmic battle for Good versus Evil? The answer is perhaps, but only as fellow travelers because the philosophy of cosmic war flows most directly from religious dogmas that embrace eschatological or "end-of-time" theology, although Buddhism and Hinduism, not generally regarded as eschatological, also have spawned cosmic war. Similarly, Marxism at its peak, or even some nationalisms, while not truly "cosmic struggles," have had some of the Manichean characteristics of cosmic war. British Marxists, for instance, probably would have died for their cause in the 1930s. Russian anarchists at the turn of the 20th century also engaged in epic battles for their beliefs, including the use of suicide terrorism to further their cause. These other "isms," therefore, have encompassing worldviews that are in some respects very similar to cosmic struggles. But what distinguishes "cosmic war" from other forms of Manichean struggles is its theological underpinnings; more so, the emphasis its believers place on fighting to create conditions conducive for the eschaton — the ultimate transcendent destination.

THE MIDDLE EAST AND COSMIC WAR

For historian Juan Cole,[8] what lies between the psychological and the socio-psychological is "personal cultural capital" - a body of inherited memories, hopes, and resentments — which he considers a very important concept for understanding the conditions under which cosmic war takes root. He argues that one cannot understand the current dynamics between the Middle East and the West without considering the last hundred-plus years of history and the impact of western colonialism on the region. Cole illustrates this point by describing the French takeover of Algeria. The French rearranged society, elevating foreigners and lowly Berbers to the top of the social ladder and relegating the clergy and old, established families to the bottom. This split persists in part despite independence, with the children of oil company executives speaking French and seeking schooling in Paris while the majority of the population receives the leftovers. This story is not unique to the Middle East where most countries have been ruled by the West for 200 years. It is also the reality in Africa and most of Asia. The genocide in Rwanda, for example, can be traced to Belgian efforts to "rearrange" society.

The Al-Qaeda worldview also reflects the history of colonialism and Christian invasion of Muslim lands — themes emphasized by its leader bin-Laden in almost all his public pronouncements and fatwahs. The Middle East, as well as the rest of the Muslim world, has been invaded by the West and humiliated and divided. While the consolidation of Europe into a set of nation-states continued in the nineteenth century, notably in Germany and Italy, that consolidation was stopped in the Middle East by colonial powers. For example, the British divided Jordan and Iraq into separate states, fractionating a cultural and geographical continuum that could have become a single political entity. The same strategy was pursued between Iraq and Kuwait. Likewise, the creation of Israel is understood as the supreme example of western efforts to divide and humiliate Arabs/Muslims in the region.

Moreover, many of the existing states, such as Egypt, are "proto-Western," in their official ideology. Nasser was not a devout or practicing Muslim; he built modern day Egypt on secular nationalist ideas. During his twenty-plus years in power, he emphasized pan-Arab nationalism, an ideology that failed to address the social and economic plight of most Egyptians. Likewise, the abolition of the Caliphate in 1924 by the ultimate westernizer, Kemal Attaturk, was the end of history for the Islamists in the region. Socialism and nationalism are pagan views to all Islamists. Thus, modern Islamists seek to reverse these trends by restoring the Caliphate, eradicating the lines in the sand that divide the Muslim *umma* or world community, and expelling western invaders and their allies. They seek to "essentialize" or "totalize" Islam, stripping it of its diverse cultural and social contexts. They envision Islam as a comprehensive and stable set of beliefs and practices that determines social, economic, and political attitudes and behavior. Moreover, Islamists argue that Islam is not a private religion, but a comprehensive ideological system covering all aspects of the state, economy, and society.

Yet many events are coded differently in the Muslim world than in the United States. For Cole, the struggle of the Palestinians to regain their lost land from the "Zionist" occupiers has been an Al-Qaeda priority. As early as the 1990s, and in particular with his 1998 fatwah, bin-Laden referred to the occupation of the holy cities, Jerusalem in particular, and called on all Muslims to kill Americans and their allies, and declared that "it is an individual duty for every Muslim who can do it in any country in which it is possible." The occupation of Jerusalem is one of many "Western" invasions; the focus is on the occupation of holy places, not the denial of rights to the Palestinians. Only later were the rights of Palestinians made an issue by Al-Qaeda.

Another key element of the Al-Qaeda view is that the United States, a champion of secularism and "Western" values, is a "paper tiger" that cut and ran in both Lebanon and Somalia. This observation inspired the strategy that the way to get at the corrupt regimes in the Middle East and return the region to a prior Islamic glory is to hit at their external support, the United States. Thus, the United States is transformed into an "enemy" of Islam. Once attacked, the United States will flee the region, leaving its puppet governments weak and vulnerable.

Secularism as championed by the United States is perceived among Islamists as an alien ideology that undermines the "purity" of Islamic values and culture. Hence it should be resisted. Because this vision of the "enemy of Islam" is unlikely to be realized in the short term, it is placed in cosmic terms as an epic battle of Good versus Evil in which the survival of the faith is at stake. According to the Islamists, the outcome of the struggle for the soul of Islam is preordained: the winner will be "Islamic culture" in the sense of it constituting a comprehensive and properly dominant world tradition.

Cole is quick to point out that these movements can go too far in the pursuit of their objectives by adopting stridently militant actions and, in so doing become their own worst enemies. For example, when Islamists' attempts to overthrow the Egyptian government were serious enough to induce the arrest of 30,000 people in the 1990s, the arrests prompted sympathy within Egypt's population and lent support for the Islamist movement. However, the massacre of 66 tourists at Luxor in 1997 evoked a very different response from the majority of Egyptians. It turned many of them against the Islamist extremists; the act, portrayed on television and condemned around the world, was horrifying and drove passive and active supporters away from the movement. Eventually even the group responsible for the Luxor massacre recanted. Therefore, these movements may find it difficult to sustain support and sympathy for the cosmic war vision over the long haul.

ASSESSING THE COSMIC WAR CONCEPT

For religious historian Philip Jenkins, the notion of "cosmic war" is provocative but too all-encompassing. For example, the language and symbols of Irish nationalism, or of the Socialist International, or of the Book of Revelation in the Bible, according to Jenkins, would translate easily into Islamist radicalism. The narrative is universal and human, not particular and Islamic.

The universal narrative of these ideologies begins with the fact that we will all die, that man is not immortal. Living conditions and life generally are bad and are getting worse because evil rules. And evil rules because of our departure from the prescribed ways. In the Muslim reality, there is a growing sense of "relative deprivation" compared with other societies. This is added to the exhaustion and disgust at the string of failed promises, failed secular or liberal solutions from Arab nationalism to Islamic socialism. What gives these ideologies appeal and a feeling of hope is the fact that there will be an enormous battle, and that we (or God) will prevail, ushering in a new order. This narrative is the human condition, not essentially an Islamic or Christian or even religious one.

However, is there something more immediate to the human condition that explains why evil rules? Here, too, the narrative is universal. This explanation locates the problem within the human domain. Evil rules because there are false prophets in the world. And these false prophets deceive us through their teachings and prophetic interpretations. Groups such as Al-Qaeda are able to exploit the paranoia inherent to this worldview.

Moreover, Jenkins observes that this type of apocalyptic worldview is not merely a non-western phenomenon; it is present in the United States as well. The Christian Identity theology, for example, a right-wing religious movement, is one of several "belief systems" in the

United States that fit this description. Its basic tenet is that the twelve tribes of ancient Israel were Caucasians who migrated to Europe shortly after the crucifixion of Jesus. Identity Christians are comprised of several variants, but one important group believes that "non-White races evolved from animals and are categorized as subhumans," and that the "biblical covenants apply only to the White race."[9] Their intense hatred for Jews and Judaism is expressed in language calling for a battle between the "true" tribe of Israel and its enemies.

Jenkins also notes that the religious extremist right in the United States and radical Islamists share a common vision. Both reject secularism and modernity, both find Judaism a major problem, and both subscribe to the use of violence and share an apocalyptic vision. And both embrace escalating religious rhetoric. In the case of the Islamists though, this rhetoric is quite often translated into violent action. *The Turner Diaries* — a book written by William Pierce, a man often identified with the Christian Identity movement in the United States but in fact the creator of Cosmotheism, based on an evolution of Nazi thought — ends with an Islamic invasion to kill all Israelis. The Vigilantes of Christ, or the Phineas movement, share a kindred vision that would be familiar to the most extreme Islamic militants.

Militant Christians and Muslims are also equally suspicious about present-day governments and their motives. The Christian Identity movement sees government as the servant of evil; it is a force designed to undermine and corrupt the faithful. This is very similar to Egyptian Islamists' views toward Nasser or Sadat, in which they consider him a "Pharaoh," someone foreign and heretical who is out to undermine the faith. Both groups also reject change, preferring the old traditional ways and values. For many Identity Christians, it is their unrelenting efforts to recapture some idealized element of America's past. They look at change through the lens of political eschatology; there are cosmic consequences if they fail to restore White America. And for the Islamists, it is the restoration of the Caliphate, one transcendent Islam with no man-made borders or geographical boundaries.

For the Identity movement, Washington is ZOG, the Zionist Occupation Government; all is deception. The more something appears in the media, the more it is untrue. And success and failure are defined in terms that Al-Qaeda would understand. Utter failure now, like losing the Battle of Algiers to French forces, may only detonate the next phase.

Holding these views alone, however, does not automatically translate into religious violence, but it does beg the question: What turns passive support into armed struggle? And what turns isolated struggle into serious war?

In cosmic war, violence is reactionary — "they" started it. But it is also active in its confrontation with evil. It doesn't need to be justified because justification is inherent in defensive action. If there is a "market for martyrs," that requires a demand, not just a supply. In Islam, for example, there is a long tradition of martyrdom that predates the command of Ayatollah Khomeini when he declared that martyrdom is "more binding to the Muslim than the command to sacrifice life and property to defend and bolster Islam."[10]

It is also important to stress that cosmic war does not predetermine a particular set of military tactics. Groups are likely to adopt the tactics that have been most successful for them, ranging from direct attacks to suicide bombings. The Tamil Tigers, for example, have engaged in suicide bombing, but they are neither Islamic nor apocalyptic. Soldiers, including American ones, die in defense of and belief in their country. Yet neither Christianity nor orthodox Islam sanctions suicide, and both are skeptical of "voluntary martyrdom." Islam expressly forbids ordinary suicide or *intihar* caused by personal distress. But *istishhad* or martyrdom is acceptable and Islamists make this distinction when justifying their use of suicide attacks.

Terrorism often "works"; it is the "poor man's response" to socio-economic and political grievances. It worked in Algeria against the French after decades of protracted violence. It worked in southern Lebanon when Israel failed to crush the Hizbollah fighters and was eventually forced to retreat. Perhaps the success of these groups is more dependent on how feasible the terrorists' goals are and the level of commitment they bring to their cause. Yet goals can dissipate quickly, or, as Algeria showed, impossible goals may become believable over time. Even the September 11th attacks shed some hope for those locked in a cosmic war with the United States. The attacks demonstrated the vulnerability of this military behemoth. It showed that a small group of determined "suicide" attackers could wreak havoc on the world's sole superpower. It succeeded in drawing the United States into a war in Afghanistan and Iraq. And it forced the United States to dramatically redirect its attention to other foreign and domestic policy goals.

Whether Al-Qaeda seeks still more devastating attacks against the United States continues to be a debated point. In one view, such attacks do not make sense, for too much killing will harden us against them. On the other hand, it is argued that Al-Qaeda wants to kill as many people as possible. And its rationale for wanting to kill Americans remains steadfast: U.S. refusal to withdraw its forces from "Muslim holy places," in other words, Saudi Arabia and Iraq, and U.S. unqualified support for Israel. The terrorists see America through the prism of Somalia and Lebanon: It is not necessary to kill too many Americans, for they do not have the "stomach" for a long, protracted war and will cut and run from the Muslim world.

Finally, is democracy the answer to cosmic war? Can democracy stem the rising tide of religiously motivated conflicts? To work, democracy has to be accepted by the losers, a demanding condition. The late Israeli scholar, Ehud Sprinzak, argues that only repression can succeed in diminishing terrorism because repression denies terrorism any hope. However, religiously inspired terrorism may not be so easily extirpated through state repression. For Cole, in the long run the autocrats are vulnerable as well. He believes that democracy can help if it is not the tyranny of the majority. That said, open societies and easy movement of goods and people — the hallmarks of a democracy — probably do facilitate terrorism.

COSMIC WAR'S IMPLICATIONS FOR INTELLIGENCE AND POLICY

For one intelligence professional, the notion of cosmic war de-mystifies a good portion of the religious violence in the world today. It is not an abstract theological concept but rather provides a framework for understanding this rising phenomenon, a dangerous reality of the new century. "Normal" people see the world in very different ways, and while cosmic war is terrifying, it is not illogical. It makes sense to its perpetrators as a rational reaction to a world estranged from God. Soldiers fight and die for their country, defending an idea or a cause, and cosmic warriors also die for their cause. Moreover, the notion enables comparison from different incidents of violence from around the world. And this comparative approach to the study of violent incidents further enhances one's understanding of terrorists' motivations. Finally, distinguishing cosmic war from other forms of war such as class or ethnic war points toward different approaches, both for intelligence analysis and for policy formulation.

However, not all spiritual conflicts can be classified as cosmic or become cosmic. The fight or struggle between Good and Evil is a major theme in nearly all religions and can remain internal to individuals. However, when the struggle becomes external, when it is linked with the social, political, and economic world around them, it then takes on cosmic dimensions. In that sense, perhaps, it would be useful to distinguish between the terrorists' core and their wider set of supporters. Perhaps we can be more successful in "de-satanizing" ourselves among the supporters, even if we can never change the minds of the core.

How can analysts know that cosmic war is afoot? Several conditions are crucial. First, warriors must regard the war as defensive, and fundamentally about identity, pride and dignity. In order to counter this type of threat, the struggle must be blocked, with more customary or attainable solutions either not sought or not within reach. Furthermore, for the "cosmic" warriors, losing the war is unthinkable; it may not be won in this generation or the next, but victory is inevitable. Cosmic war, therefore, is endless, for the struggle between Good and Evil has no end. Finally, cosmic war is exciting and fulfilling, it gives purpose to a group's struggle, it carries a divine imprimatur, and while it looks horrible to us, it is definitely positive for the warriors and gives them an opportunity to regain their dignity.

Where should analysts expect cosmic war? Surely there is all too much fertile ground for it in poor countries, especially in the zones of religious fracture — the conflict between Israel and the Palestinians, or Sunnis and Shias, or in the Sahel and North Africa. It is also present in parts of Asia and has the potential to rear its head in Central Asia. But several cases also show that cosmic war can be found in western societies as well, including the United States. While geographic location is important, it is an understanding of the political eschatology of cosmic war and its dissemination that should be of more concern to the intelligence analyst.

How can cosmic war be addressed? The observation that using force often backfires is important to keep in mind. Force is a limited tool, not a blanket approach for dealing with every type of conflict. It is one arrow, albeit a strong one, in a state's quiver. The U.S. declaration of a "war on terrorism" after the September 11th attacks culminated in a military victory later that year that toppled the Taliban regime in Afghanistan, demolishing Al-Qaeda training facilities and safe havens. Still, that war was at best only partially successful. Al-Qaeda and its network of non-state actors, religious motivated warriors, remains the greatest threat to the United States. Mark Juergensmeyer advances the point that "the U.S. government's own assessment made clear that its violent assault against al Qaeda — the largest military operation ever conducted against a non-state activist network — was of only limited success."[11] Ideally, we could try to break up cells of warriors without the use of overwhelming force. If we could, too, we should try to separate the religious from the purely political. So, too, we should try to defuse support for the warriors by gaining the moral high ground.

Steven Simon, a former National Security Council official dealing with terrorism and the co-author of *The Age of Sacred Terror*, observes that if the experts could not agree on Al-Qaeda's objectives or motives, what hope was there for intelligence analysis?[12] Surely, the first task is to comprehend the cosmic dimension of Al-Qaeda's struggle against the West. Failing to see that would ineluctably lead to faulty analysis.

Simon presents another view of cosmic war. According to him, cosmic war is gnostic in inspiration. The world is in the grip of a demigod, one who is different from the godhead. That demigod deceives, keeping us all in a state of confusion and bafflement. What appears to be life on earth is in fact a prison. If only we had the secret knowledge, the Gnosis, we would break out and "end history."

For Simon, the compelling issue facing the United States is how policy can address cosmic war when, by definition, anything the United States says is a lie? Moreover, the warriors conceive of themselves as a threatened enclave, God's chosen servants with an end-of-time message. Can the United States government engage in dialogue with a religious interlocutor? Can it do "faith-based diplomacy"? And if it can, should it? The policy agenda outlined by Juergensmeyer is sensible but difficult to implement. The difficulty, it would seem, stems more from too little understanding of cosmic war and a lack of political will to change policy directions than from a desire for dialogue. We don't want to reaffirm the agenda of the cosmic warriors, yet we must face the fact that all we say is immediately dismissed as a lie or deception.

In practice, the government has found it difficult to frame the message beyond "the war on terror is not a war on Islam," and even that message has been dismissed or overwhelmed. Several of the government's pronouncements against Al-Qaeda, against the "extremists" or radical "fundamentalists," are also couched in "cosmic" terms that make it increasingly difficult for any side to extricate itself from the struggle. There is, at the same time, a feedback loop between what we say and what they say they want. When we say what scares us, they notice, and they reflect our projected concerns.

As an intelligence matter, Simon suggests, while the boundaries appear nebulous and tricky at times, we should pay closer attention to religious language, to its style and substance, its historical context and symbolic content, its deeper meanings and cultural moorings. All these can be very potent and very useful in intelligence analysis. We should be far more sensitive to the use of apocalyptic language by particular groups. And we should also look for the language of dream, or repentance, or sudden change of fortune. If weapons of mass destruction (WMD) are described in instrumental terms, then deterrence may still be possible. If, however, the language is apocalyptic, if it paints a transcendent picture, then we enter another realm.

Analysis should not pay too much attention to attributes of personal piety, particularly when examining Islam in Europe. Muslims there can be a great threat to the United States. They do not see themselves as Europeans, but Muslims first and their "ancestral" identity second. While the younger generation was born in Europe and has adopted Western mores and cultural trappings more so than their parents, that generation has, nevertheless, demonstrated a strong affinity toward their Islamic roots. This condition has been greatly exacerbated by what they perceive to be "America's war against Islam," not terrorism. Many European and American Muslims may not be pious in practice, but are attracted to a heterodox Islam, a jihadist Islam that destroys all, including the laws of its own faith, to make way for a new order.

Many of them are first generation migrants, especially in continental Europe, but older migrants are also converted. British officials estimate that 10,000 in Britain have converted to Islam in the last three years. In policy terms, that suggests a very broad conversation between the United States and Europe, one that ranges far from law enforcement to the conditions that may spawn or inhibit dangerous threats. More broadly, processes of secularization tend to be a dropping out, an individualization; sacralization tends to be a joining up, a collectivization.

If conversion to Islam in Europe is a concern, so, too, is it in the United States. There has been a "rediscovery of roots," particularly among Iranians in the United States, and conversions in prison, especially among blacks and Latinos, have turned prisons into veritable recruiting posts for Al-Qaeda networks.

Finally, Simon notes that there has been a real debate in Salafi Islam over the limits of killing. A November 2002 Al-Qaeda statement provoked a reaction about killing women and children and led some Islamic leaders to draw something akin to a distinction between combatants and non-combatants. Osama bin-Laden agreed but argued that since the United States is a democracy, all its citizens deserve death for electing George Bush, who they assert, is waging a war against Islam.

Attacks on children are a distinct possibility. Again, the logic for Jihadists would be defensive, a retaliation for Arab and Muslim children already killed. Al-Qaeda statements are worrisome in emphasizing the depredations the West has inflicted on Islam's children. Pictures of dead Muslim children killed and maimed by U.S. and Israeli bombs may be a "money shot" for Al Jazeera, though, plainly, gruesome images can also turn off would-be supporters.

3. STATES AND RELIGIOUS VIOLENCE

Building on the concept of cosmic war, this section explores the conditions under which religiously motivated violence and terrorism arise. Specifically, it considers the role of governments in exacerbating cosmic war and tools that the state has and can use for managing religious violence. It begins by applying the notion of 20th century Italian socialist Antonio Gramsci of a political "war of position" to religious violence and terrorism. It then proposes a model for defining and distinguishing different types of religious fundamentalism, paying particular attention to the conditions under which religious fundamentalists become violent. Third, it offers a case study to illustrate these concepts, looking at the Islamic Republic of Iran. Fourth, it considers the United State's response to the September 11th attacks and how this has affected and influenced Al-Qaeda, along with other policy and intelligence implications.

"POLITICAL WARS OF POSITION" BETWEEN STATES AND RELIGION

Political scientist Ian Lustick argues that Lenin's question about politics is highly relevant when thinking about religious violence and the state: Who is the "who," (the actor) and who is the "whom" (the acted upon)?[13] Gramsci elaborated the distinction.[14]

To illustrate this point, Lustick describes the dynamics between Rabbi Kook, the British-appointed chief rabbi in Palestine, and British authorities occupying the country. Unlike other rabbis, Rabbi Kook was a Zionist, viewing God as acting through the kibbutzniks, socialist settlers who ate pork and violated other religious norms but still considered themselves Jewish. He joined forces with the secular-socialist leader Ben Gurion, and so became a "whom"; he was used by the secular nationalists to eventually create a secular Jewish state.

However, decades later seventeen graduates of his yeshiva became leaders of Gush Emunim (Block of the Faithful), a radical religious Jewish organization bent on absorbing the West Bank, Gaza Strip, Golan Heights and East Jerusalem into Eretz Yisrael, greater Israel. In justifying their case, they have "cited the Torah to define the boundaries of their Israel and to inspire militant policies and actions."[15] It was then that the secular-minded Labor Party, which first supported the religious settlers but then grew to regret it, became the "whom," used by Gush Emunim to further its religious agenda. In a similar way, one line of fundamentalist Christians in the United States and Jewish fundamentalists in Israel now support one another even though they are diametrically opposed; each views the other as useful for achieving its own religious goals.

Lustick further elaborates the "who/whom" distinction, drawing on Gramsci, who outlined three forms of political struggle that apply to religious violence and the state. The first, in fixed regimes, is normal politics about elections. The second occurs when there is disagreement about the rules of the road. The third is competition over the boundaries of political groups, what might be called "political wars of position." Gramsci's third category is particularly useful for understanding, on the one hand, which states use religion for political gain and in what ways they do it, and on the other, whether and how religions may use states for religious gain.

Lustick observes that, in the United States, it is not permissible to conduct wars of position over race, class, or religion. This is not to say that attempts have not been made by political parties to stake out positions over these issues, but those attempts stop short of engaging in "a war of position." However, governments elsewhere have been tempted to use these issues in wars against their main political opponents. For example, the rightwing Israeli party, Likud, formed an alliance with Jewish religious movements in order to defeat the leftwing opposition, the Labor Party, in the 1977 general elections. This brought religion and religious agendas into the Israeli government in new ways.

Lustick further argues that most Middle Eastern states have entered into a bargain with the devil. While they have prevented the Islamists from taking power legally, and in some instances crushed them, they have, at the same time tolerated a kind of organized rebellion, which can be considered as a political war of position. In a few of those states, such as Jordan, that war was conducted in the social sphere, where the Islamists were permitted to compete with other socio-political forces. In contrast, other states — such as Algeria, Tunisia, and Syria — refused to make this bargain, and instead attempted to eradicate the Islamist voice altogether.

DEFINING THE DYNAMICS OF FUNDAMENTALISM

As a descriptive term for capturing ideologically oriented religious movements, religious fundamentalism is often equated with violent extremism, religious militancy, and terrorism. Secular fundamentalism, on the other hand, is manifested in Marxism and in the many virulent strains of anti-clerical nationalism. The two forms are distinguishable because of the authentic "religious" nature of religious fundamentalism. In its original usage, though, fundamentalism was accurately applied to those Protestant Christians of North America who coined the term in the 1920s, and later to their ideological heirs. The concept of fundamentalism can best be viewed through the lens of comparative constructs that help us to differentiate patterns of activism. This comparative approach defines fundamentalism as "a discernible pattern of religious militancy by which self-styled 'true believers' attempt to arrest the erosion of religious identity, fortify the borders of the religious community, and create viable alternatives to secular institutions and behaviors."[16]

Religious fundamentalists are generally viewed as doctrinaire followers of sacred scripture, dwellers in and on the past, and involved in what they see as a life and death struggle between Good and Evil.[17] In a broader sense, fundamentalism refers to an orientation to the world, one that inheres both a cognitive and an emotional dimension. Its ethos is one of protest and outrage at the secularization of society - that is, at the process by which religion and its spirit have been steadily removed from public life. It is important to note that very few individuals who are accurately branded as "fundamentalist" actually participate in acts of terror and violence. Most fundamentalists are struggling to live a religious life as they see it in a world that seems increasingly inimical to faith.

So what then is fundamentalism? To be sure, fundamentalism is not a monolithic idea or movement that expresses or adheres to a single set of ideals. It is not simply extremism or conservatism. Billy Graham, for example, would not be accepted as a fundamentalist by all those Christians who call themselves fundamentalists, nor would he call himself one. Fundamentalism is not the same as traditionalism. Rather, fundamentalism is "a kind of revolt or rebellion against the secular hegemony of the modern world. Fundamentalists typically want to see God, or religion, reflected more centrally in public life. They want to drag religion from the sidelines, to which it's been relegated in a secular culture, and back to center stage."[18] For those who see themselves as Muslim fundamentalists, it is a reaction to militant secularism. And for others, it represents a strong desire to see religion reflected more clearly in their polity.

In examining fundamentalism, Lustick moves beyond "wars of position" as an instrument for understanding states' use of religion. He also argues that taxonomy is useful when examining the concept of religious violence. He proposes that fundamentalism should be differentiated in three ways: a call for a radical, rapid and comprehensive transformation of society; a belief that there is some direct link between adherents and the ultimate source of authority in the cosmos, making compromise difficult; and a call to be *active* in the political realm.

Different approaches along each of the three dimensions mentioned above would yield distinct results. For instance, pietism may seek dramatic changes in society and cultivate a direct link to God, but at the same time it tends to shun politics.

Examples of high-medium-high ranking groups include the charismatic leader Rabbi Kook, who has passed from the scene to leave his vanguard of disciples to argue about the true path. Or, in Israel, high-high-medium might be the ultra-Orthodox haredim, pietists who originally were low-high-medium but have been radicalized.

Table 2 ranks Israeli religious groups as high or medium on the three dimensions:

Table 2

Fundamentalist Variants: Israeli Example

	Radical	Direct	Politics
Gush Emunim with Rav Kook; consensus builders vs. vanguardists	High	High	High
Vanguardists in charge; threat of disastrous miscalculation	High	Medium	High
Temple Mount haredim; threat of pietistic retreat/"blackening"	High	High	Medium
Consensus-Builders in charge: threat of cooptation; depends on charismatic leader to prevent schism	Medium	High	High

Fundamentalism's advantages are certainty and sacrifice; both of these advantages give it the edge during crises. This also suggests that its leaders will try to define moments as scary and classify them as apocalyptic crises, arguing that religion is the answer. Thus, the passing of its charismatic leader can cause grave problems, especially if the mantle of leadership has not been passed before the leader dies. If Iraq's Shia are high-high-high under Ayatollah Sistani and he dies before naming a successor, then what? Moving to high-medium-high could lead to factional in-fighting, while moving toward medium-medium-high would be politicized pietism. The key to understanding how the Shia would change is to understand the starting point: How radical are the Shia now?

LEARNING FROM THE IRAN CASE

Historian Juan Cole argues that, for all its problems, Iran's theocracy is not yet a plain failure, so it is a case worth examining both in its own right and as a guide to the future of Iraq. This case is undoubtedly the most dramatic example of politics and religion (Islam) in the 20h century. The cataclysmic change brought about in 1978-1979 has fueled, more than any other, the American image of radical or fundamentalist Islam.

Cole proposes that states are pragmatic and thus resist engaging in cosmic war, which is costly and, ultimately, cannot be won. However, when states do use religious war, they do so for their own non-religious purposes. The United States, for example, used many religious groups during the Cold War, including the mujahideen in Afghanistan. In the early 1970s, radical Islamism was looked upon kindly by the Western block, and Middle Eastern regimes contending with leftist oppositions broadly encouraged their bearded Islamist students. While Washington did not believe in their religious motivations or share their radical interpretations of religion, it did find them useful for confronting Soviet expansionism and communism, particularly in Third World conflict arenas.

The cases in which states are ideologically linked to cosmic war, and are themselves revolutionary and are much rarer, which makes Iran in the 1980s all the more interesting. Cole notes that Khomeini fits Lustick's definition of a "fundamentalist," which is not the usual way Shia clerics are viewed. Political rule by clerics was a Khomeini-inspired innovation in Shiism. It represented a radical departure from the "quietism" adopted and practiced by Shias for hundreds of years. Shias were taught to refrain from political discourses, to keep their religion separate from politics. Khomeini's message was appealing as it combined religion, nationalism, and populism. Cole further explains that Shia Islam believes that Ali, the son-in-law of Muhammad, was the blood-designated successor to the Prophet and that he would act as both the spiritual and political leader of all Muslims. This event, long held sacred by all Shias, was given a "unique" interpretation by Ali Shari'ati, an Iranian Ph.D. from the Sorbonne, whose writings inspired Khomeini's revolutionary views.

Shari'ati "presented a Shia Islam that was liberating and revolutionary by positing a distinction between 'Alid' and 'Safavid' Islam. The former was the pure Islam personified by Ali. . . . What Shari'ati called Safavid Islam, by contrast, was the debased, quietist, and obscurantist Islam cobbled together by later clerics."[19] Shari'ati's reformulation gave Shia Islam a revolutionary fervor that Khomeini fully embraced. Authority would pass to Ali's descendants, who were called "Imams" or leaders. However, when the twelfth Imam disappeared, the Shias were left with no legitimate authority.

Most Shias were taught to believe that the clergy is empowered to make everyday social and religious decisions but not political ones. Khomeini, however, believed that the clergy should not only have a say in spiritual life but should also play a major role in politics. In his most famous writing, *Islamic Government*, Khomeini preached:

> You must make yourselves known to the people of the world and also authentic models of Islamic leadership and government. You must address yourselves to the university people in particular, the educated class. . . . The students are looking to Najaf, appealing for help. Should we sit idle, waiting for them to enjoin the good upon us and call us to our duties?[20]

He authorized the clergy to rule politically and advocated that theocratic rule, as a general model, was the best means of government, even beyond Islam. The political agenda delineated from Khomeini's Islamic government can be simply stated: "Islam provides a comprehensive sociopolitical system valid for all time and place. Thus, God is the sole legislator. Government is mandated in order to implement God's plan in this world. Individual believers are not permitted simply to suffer unjust rule in silence. They must actively work to realize God's plan in this world. The only acceptable form of this Islamic government is that directed by the most religiously learned. This is the guardianship of the faqih (velayat-e-faqih)."[21]

In some respects, Khomeini was almost a Leninist, making clerics the revolutionary cadre. According to one analyst, "Khomeini is to the Islamic Revolution what Lenin was to the Bolshevik, Mao to the Chinese, and Castro to the Cuban revolutions."[22] The success of Khomeini in fomenting his vision of revolution lay, in part, in his ability to relate his ideology to a diverse set of interest groups. He possessed both ideology and organization. And his message carried widespread appeal, not only to the clerics but also to students, professionals, and the *bazaari* merchants. In this sense, the Iranian revolution was really a series of micro revolutions within disparate segments of the population under the rubric of the Khomeini revolution.

When Khomeni called on Iraqi Shias to emulate Iran following the 1979 revolution, Saddam Hussein responded with repression toward the Shias in Iraq, and many fled to Iran where they established the Supreme Council for Islamic Revolution in Iraq (SCIRI).

During the Lebanese Civil war, several Shia groups, supported by Tehran, sprang up with the aim of gaining greater rights for their constituents, including AMAL (which later became Islamic AMAL), and its offshoot, Hizbollah, which was openly Khomeini-ist and agitated for an Iranian-style revolution.

After Khomeini's death in 1989, however, Iran backed off from its radicalism somewhat, although it continued to support the Lebanese Hizbollah in its efforts to drive Israel out of Lebanon.

In Iran, the Khomeini-ists were voted out in fair elections in 1997, when 70 percent of the population elected the moderate Khatami. Although the Khomeini-ists' popular support has declined to perhaps 15 percent of the population, they nevertheless retain key levers of power, winning the last elections in February 2004 only by excluding 4,000 candidates. Fairer elections strongly indicate that fewer and fewer clerics would be elected in the future, and with women and the young (15-year olds) now able to exercise the franchise, it means further erosion of the clerics' hold on political power.

Following the U.S. led invasion of Iraq and the capture of Saddam Hussein in December 2003, Iraqi Shias have returned from Iran and from London, the latter a more moderate stream of exiles. Cole estimates that perhaps 20 to 30 percent of Iraqi Shias are Khomeini-ist. The Grand Ayatollah al-Sistani, the most revered of Iraqi Shia clerics, is not an Islamist extremist. His is a moderate position with an aversion to mixing religion and politics. While he is not calling for radical changes, he does favor something like the role of the Catholic Church in Ireland in the 1950s — a veto over government actions bearing on the religious and social sphere, which he has interpreted broadly. If Sistani were to be killed or to die from natural causes given his frail health, the other three Grand Ayatollahs in Iraq are also relatively moderate, though one, a Pakistani by nationality, is anti-American.

The young radical Shia cleric, Muqtada al-Sadr, and his followers, however, are religious extremists and, while they constitute a minority of Shias in Iraq, they do have a strong base of support (over 2 million followers) in Sadr City, east of Baghdad, and in the south of the country. The question is, therefore: Where do Shias go for politico-religious leadership, Sistani and the other clerics in Najaf or Sadr and his followers? And what should the United States do to cultivate closer relations with al-Sistani and encourage the propagation of his moderate views?

U.S. RESPONSES TO THE AL-QAEDA THREAT: IMPLICATIONS FOR POLICY AND INTELLIGENCE

RAND analyst Steven Simon argues that September 11th was a massive act of political theater, aimed at defining the terms of engagement, at reorganizing the grand war of position so that the world would see the antinomian struggle between Good and Evil as one pitting Islam against its only worthy opponent, the Great Satan, the United States. Osama bin-Laden thus wrote the script for both Afghanistan and Iraq. This is drama. And as drama, hurting the United States is not enough. Anthrax scare or sniper attacks by disgruntled "locals" do not suffice, no matter how much these events might hurt the U.S. economy. The dramatists need greater acts, more stupendous and spectacular, greater sacrifice from the perpetrators, and they need to keep the drama going.

Simon further argues that, while the drama is critical, while it has life-and-death consequences, it is only one element of the struggle; there is also an operational/strategic component. Prior to September 11th, Al-Qaeda and its Cairo networks had attempted to overthrow the corrupt and "un-Islamic" governments in Egypt and Saudi Arabia but had been thwarted, in their view, by the enemy from afar, the United States. America's continued support for these countries, in spite of their human rights abuses and suppression of dissent, served to inflame the radicals' posture toward the United States. They argued that, in order to succeed at home, they had to take on the distant enemy that was propping up their "corrupt" regimes at home; they had to get the United

States out of the way, just as Japan intended in World War II when its real imperial target was not North America but Asia.

The September 11th attacks could have been intended to induce an overreaction by the United States against the Muslim world, and the terrorists might have achieved this objective with the U.S. invasions of Afghanistan and Iraq.

Seen in dramatic terms, then, what is the next target? It might be the White House or the Capitol Building, or it could be other symbols of America's economic and financial power. The experience in Somalia would suggest another sort of precedent, perhaps for U.S. involvement in Iraq: If the United States can be drawn into a protracted conflict and beaten like the Soviets in Afghanistan, then it will be knocked out for good.

Are there identifiable actions by the state that lead to cosmic war? Developments in Israel and Iran suggest possible triggers to cosmic war. Religious parties moved to the fore in Israel only after the secular, socialist experiments failed. In Iran, Khomeini came to power only after another secular, modernizing experiment became discredited, even for the very Iranians who had seemed to benefit most from the Shah's rule.

For individual cosmic warriors, striking out may be the first act before they turn to a war of position. States, slow to see cosmic war as a mortal threat, deal with the warriors tactically. Secular approaches may work for several decades or even a half-century, but states' lack of tools in the spiritual-ideological realm is a weakness in dealing with cosmic war.

Thus, it is important to reiterate that cosmic war need not stem from purely religious causes, a point made in the first section. Whatever its causes, it is always present at some level, and so the question is: What detonates it?

So far, the cases of cosmic warriors taking over governments are only two, the Taliban and Khomeini. Khomeini is a reminder that all revolutions are multiple; he used a broad-based message to rally oil workers, students, Islamists, and others to his revolution. The Taliban, on the other hand, restored order to a country wracked by protracted ethnic and tribal conflict.

Simon suggests that, from a policy perspective, the French word *engrenage*, or gears meshing, describes the militants' overall strategy. The adversary seeks to force the state to mesh with it in particular ways, compelling it to take actions it would prefer to avoid. In other words, both parties' actions force a reaction from the other, propelling the conflict forward.

Moreover, extremists and some fundamentalists may also combine cosmic war with more "normal" politics. Members of Hizbollah sit in the Lebanese parliament but also engage in terror in the south. This might be a trend in Iraq as well.

Simon notes that cognitive bias is an obstacle to both policy and understanding. The United States is a secular state, at least in its government, and it has struggled to fully grasp or understand the reasons behind Al-Qaeda's religious motivations. For example, the U.S. government described the Bali bombing as "economic war" when clearly religion and other motivating factors were behind it. This consistent lack of understanding blunts appropriate responses. Simon opined that this description has prompted Al-Qaeda to react to our signal of vulnerability, and it has begun talking of economic war.

Simon further asserts that "norm entrepreneurs" help people see hypocrisy, thus creating cognitive dissonance. Those entrepreneurs are "gnostics," telling people that things are not what they seem. Similarly, Lustick observes that Gush Emunim talks of the secret below the public discourse, the secret that was too much to be openly ventilated. The desire of some in the movement to annex biblical sites in the West Bank, Gaza Strip, Golan Heights, East Jerusalem, and Lebanon was the "truth" that was a "noise too great for the ear to hear." So although they suppressed that language from their public discourse, it remains a staple in their internal debate. Analysts need to be sensitive to such language on the parts of potential cosmic warriors and of governments that resort to the same tactic.

For Iraq, while majoritarian politics might spawn quasi-ethnic wars between Shias and Sunni, it is worth remembering that ethnic conflict is not the same as cosmic war. However, in addition to the potential for ethnic or regional wars in Iraq, cosmic war is also possible, particularly with Zarqawi and al-Sadr trying to light the fire. These leaders perceive the struggle against the United States in cosmic terms.

The Israeli-Palestinian conflict is essentially a political struggle, but it has the potential to take on a cosmic dimension, especially as militant religious groups, such as the Islamic Hamas and the Jewish Gush Emunim continue to cast the conflict in religious terms. For now, advancing the Israel-Palestine issue seems extremely difficult for the United States. This is so largely because of America's overwhelming support for Israel and its right to exist as an independent Jewish state. In this struggle, Arabs and Muslims see the United States not as an honest broker for peace but as completely partial and untrustworthy. If this common but for now localized perception should become transformed into one in which the United States is seen as an enemy of Islam, then this conflict could truly have cosmic implications. The present impasse plays too well into Al-Qaeda's propaganda machine. Therefore, the Israeli-Palestinian conflict is one problem that the United States cannot afford to leave unsolved, no matter how difficult or improbable a solution may seem to be at this point.

4. SCANNING FOR NEW RELIGIOUS MOVEMENTS

This section explores a number of new or newly salient religious groups, groups that are commonly referred to as New Religious Movements (NRMs), and specifically investigates which movements turn violent, as only a few do. It begins, first, by outlining several definitions of NRMs and how they might be distinguished from traditional religions. Second, it explores the conditions under which NRMs turn violent. It then offers a case study, looking at the Sadr movement in Iraq as an example of a new NRM. Fourth, it compares examples of NRMs in Christianity and Islam. And, finally, it concludes by scanning the horizon for the emergence of violent NRMs.

DEFINING NRMs

The definition of NRMs is not universally agreed upon; the term itself is an exercise in political correctness, seeking to avoid the connotations of "cult." Recent incidences of mass suicide, homicide, and terrorism have renewed interest in religious movements as opposed to violent movements claiming to be part of the "old" religions such as Judaism, Islam, and evangelical Protestantism. Religious violence by those "old" religions was largely ignored during the controversies surrounding cults, a controversy that came to be known in the United States as the "cult wars." Throughout the 1980s, under the label "cult," new religions went through a period of vilification; in some cases, there were challenges in court to their status. Today, the number of these NRMs has grown astronomically; one scholar estimates that there are 800 in North America alone.[23] The terms *cult* and *NRM* are used interchangeably in this report.

For historian Juan Cole, the two defining characteristics of NRMs by any name are

- a high degree of tension between the group and surrounding society; and
- a high degree of control over members exercised by leaders.

That control extends to members' finances, friends and family — indeed, to their entire lives. These movements make extreme demands on members, and often isolate those members from mainstream society. Control and leadership veneration are hallmarks of NRMs. "The role (and mental condition) of the leader of the group seems to be decisive in persuading followers either to choose the radical option, or to adjust as well as possible to adverse circumstances."[24]

There is a discernible expansion of NRMs across the global landscape, and this trend has been evident since the end of the Second World War. In the 1980s, "it burst upon the popular consciousness as the New Age Movement. . . . Literally millions of people were attracted by the vision of hope, and experienced the personal transformation which welcomed them to the movement."[25] NRMs, especially in the United States, have largely been regarded as a middle-class phenomenon; however, in societies around the world, including the United States, examples of NRMs can be found across all classes. Social dislocations, particularly in economically and politically depressed societies, can become fertile breeding grounds for NRM recruitment. For example, major social dislocations have produced NRMs in places such as Iraq, India, and Pakistan.

Philip Jenkins, a historian of religious studies, defines NRMs as groups that are charismatically led, authoritarian, puritanical, and totalistic; it is in the manipulation of boundary controls that the "totalism" becomes possible. It is worth remembering, though, that many established religions, Unitarians perhaps excepted, are both apocalyptic and millennial. Quakers, Baptists, and Methodists were regarded as dangerous when they were NRMs, but over time they became mainstream religions.

One useful model, outlined by John Lofland and Rodney Stark[26] and used in explaining cult recruitment/conversion, suggests stages of progression toward full inclusion into the movement:

- A person experiences acute and persistent tensions within his or her religious life.
- The individual defines himself or herself as a religious seeker.

- He/she then encounters the movement at a crucial turning point in life.
- The individual forms an affective bond with one or more existing convert or member.
- Extra-cult attachments become attenuated; the recruit sees less of those outside the movement while getting more involved with those inside the movement en route to full membership.
- A person feels acute and persistent internal tensions between diminished ties with old friends and family and experiences of intensive interaction within the group.
- He or she then ultimately becomes the group's deployable agent.

The process of recruitment-commitment-conversion takes new members across the boundary between mainstream society and the movement, a boundary that can be virtual or real. The new recruit first forms links over that boundary then begins to cut off links with those outside the movement, reinforcing his or her separation. The process acts much like a filter for reality. The recruits see what the group wants them to see, dress as they dress, and live with them as they live. As changes in the recruits' degree of commitment occur, they become conditioned to espousing the group's perceptions of the outside world. Apart from knowing about this "conversion" process, it is also important to understand what NRMs have in common. Most NRMs may be entirely peaceful, but we may nonetheless ask: Is there a set of common identifiable elements in their modus operandi that would drive them under certain conditions to suicide, homicide, or terrorism?

One close examination of a number of these movements, such as Solar Temple and Heaven's Gate, found that "not only did they react to perceived threats from outside, but they also propagated a theology that encouraged group members to regard themselves as 'not of this world.'"[27] It was also observed that cult members feel a "deep estrangement from the world, perceived opposition by former members well acquainted with the inner dealings of the group, threats from outside agencies (real or imaginary) and the feeling that there was no possible way to escape 'but up.'"[28]

The Christian Identity Movement illustrates both the process of incorporation into a NRM and its motivations for violence. This movement is based on a 19th-century concept known as Anglo-Israelism. Identity Christians believe that northern Europeans are the true lost tribes of Israel, the direct descendants of the "chosen" tribes of ancient Israel. They are strongly anti-Semitic, "claiming that humans originated from 'two seed lines.' Whites are directly descended from God, whereas Jews originated from an illicit sexual union between the Devil and the first white woman."[29] By their reasoning, the existing Jews are not God's true chosen people but, rather, are deceptive and evil. Evil on earth rules through deception and money. Only Identity Christians know the Truth, and it is their duty both to expose the deceit of the Jews and to defeat their alliance with the U.S. government, which they call the Zionist Occupation Government (ZOG).

An offshoot of the Christian Identity movement, called the Order, broke away because it regarded the Identity movement as ineffective. The Order brought people into its organization by seeking out disaffected white, male Christians; by running them through a series of trials to confirm their sincerity; by training members in clandestine paramilitary camps; and by hatching plans to overthrow the U.S. government and its "Zionist conspirators." Those sentiments were evident in Timothy McVeigh, the Oklahoma City bomber, who was probably too young to have been a member of the Order, which was effectively wrapped up by the government in 1984, but who reflected its views.[30]

In Europe, Islam has now taken on a distinct new role alongside other religious fringe groups. Young Europeans — white, non-ethnic and often working class — have long existed in a kind of "cult milieu," in which they can "shop" around among several cults at the same time, looking to try new experiences. They become "serial saints," what Grace Davy calls "believing without belonging." More recently, however, some, like Richard Reid, the "shoe bomber," have converted to Islam and eventually become radicalized. In Britain, for instance, mainstream Christianity is now most alive among migrant black populations from

Africa and the Caribbean; hence Christianity is perceived, especially by the young, as a "black thing."[31] In these circumstances, radical Islam has gained appeal and a large following. Beyond the usual transitional spiritual experience, it provides enemies, authority, certainty, fraternity, and an apocalyptic vision.

It is also worth noting that there are many links (including website links) between Middle Eastern radicalism and neo-Nazism, especially in Europe. They are aligned through a common enemy, namely Jews and the United States government. Jenkins notes that there is a long tradition of the former subcontracting violent attacks out to the latter.

Prisons are especially fertile recruiting grounds for NRMs because prisoners have already moved through a number of the stages outlined above, including separation from family and society, an authoritarian environment, and little control over their lives. This is particularly true in the United States, where prison populations reflect a broad cross-section of males who share similar socioeconomic backgrounds. Jenkins notes that New York State has hired Muslim chaplains who espouse the ultra-conservative Wahhabi interpretation of Islam.

The NRM concept has not been used in examining the rise of militant Islam in the Middle East. Most, if not all, of the studies on religious movements have focused on NRM activities in North America and Europe. However, foreshadowing a later discussion, Cole suggests that the Sadr movement in Iraq fits the definitions of a new religious movement in many respects. Sadr's group is millenarian; it expects the imminent return of the hidden Imam — the "divinely guided one," the one who will usher in a reign of peace and prosperity for all Shias. The belief in the coming of the hidden Imam has major ecclesiastical importance in Shia Islam.

Sadr himself is a young, inexperienced leader who is at odds with the older, more established Shia clergy in Iraq. Although his movement is on the fringe and in tension with mainstream Shia society, it has a sizable following, one not merely concentrated in Sadr City. His followers are drawn from the ranks of the young and unemployed. And his movement sprang from the harsh realities of economic deprivation, political repression, and widespread illiteracy so prevalent among the slum dwellers in eastern Baghdad. While his followers are not cosmic warriors and while the divide between followers of Sadr and Sistani is blurred, many of Sadr's followers are radicalized and will readily defend their faith against infidels.

Given this situation, it is likely that Sadr's movement can be de-radicalized if the conditions that spawned the alienation of its adherents were to improve. Can the young Sadr himself become de-radicalized if his grievances are realistically addressed? It is not clear. The death of the most senior Shia cleric in Iraq, the Grand Ayatollah Sistani, could lead to deeper fractures in the Shia community. How would his death affect Sadr's movement? While no one knows for certain, it is possible that Sadr might see this as an opportunity to enlarge his base of supporters and hence his influence. Cole surmises that it would most likely not make much of a difference, for Sistani's likely successors are cut from the same cloth and therefore would allow for continuity within mainstream Shiism in Iraq.

What about the return of the Grand Ayatollah Kazim al Hairi from Iran? He is more radical than the Ayatollahs in Iraq now and follows a religious-political agenda similar to that of Ayatollah Khomeini. But it is worth remembering that NRMs often become modified and more mainstream over time; even Khomeinism has softened over the past few decades.

WHAT INDUCES NRMs TO ENGAGE IN VIOLENCE?

How important are NRMs in thinking about the future of terrorism? Are they inclined to become major actors on the "terrorism" stage? For Jenkins, the answer is "not very." He argues that most NRMs are not violent and only very few have engaged in terrorist acts against civilians, while a few have resorted to mass suicide. However, there are lessons to be learned about existing organizations from the literature on NRMs, particularly from the ones that espouse cosmic war. The arresting images of NRM violence have been mass suicides carried out by groups such as the Order of the Solar Temple (October 1994), when Swiss police discovered 48 bodies in three chalets in Granges-sur-Salvan; Heaven's Gate, an NRM fixated on UFOs (March 1997), when 39 members committed suicide in Rancho Santa Fe, California; and the more recent suicide of 800 members of the Movement for the Restoration of the Ten Commandments of God in Uganda, March 2000. The mass suicide of groups such as the People's Temple in Jonestown, Guyana, and the Branch Davidians in Waco, Texas, are also seared into America's collective memory about NRMs and their potential for violence.

However, Jenkins argues that those suicides were more political than religious in motivation, a point that can be debated. A non-religious reason may have been the trigger, but underlying all of the suicide episodes was a powerful and compelling apocalyptic vision combined with an urgency to hasten the coming of a new world. That said, groups that score high on both of Cole's criteria for NRMs — a high degree of tension with society and a high degree of control over adherents in a movement — are not necessarily more prone toward violence. The Amish, for instance, would be an example of a group that fits this description, and yet they are definitely nonviolent. Therefore, violence on the part of NRMs seems likely to derive from conditions outside the movement.

A "psycho-pathological" view of cult violence argues that deranged leaders prey on weak or vulnerable members. It holds that no one is capable of performing such extreme acts as ritualized suicide and homicide without having been brainwashed by an evil guru or leader. While this view should be treated with caution because it is, in some sense, too easy an explanation, there has been retrospective evidence of "brainwashing" in some of the suicides.

Other explanations of why cults turn to violence would focus, first, on the possibility that they will be challenged or even attacked by mainstream society or the government. The FBI pursued very different tactics in its confrontations at Waco and Ruby Ridge, on the one hand, and with the Freeman in Montana on the other. In Waco, it assaulted the compound, leading to the deaths of nearly all those inside, including children. In contrast, with the Freemen, it sent in a steady stream of former members to negotiate with those inside, used theologically neutral language, and was patient, resolving the standoff without bloodshed.

A second factor that may lead to NRM violence is the quality of leadership within the movement. Cult leaders seem to be a special breed of people. Apart from an inflated ego and a compelling need for adulation, they are also charismatic and gifted doctrinaire persuaders of a particular worldview. If the leaders are young and inexperienced, they may be more inclined to take risks, be impulsive, and resort to violence. Moreover, if movements do not have experienced leaders, it may be more difficult for them to transfer power, causing the organizations to fall into internal schism or turmoil and possibly break up.[32]

SHIAS IN THE MIDDLE EAST AS NRMS

As noted earlier, the Sadr movement in Iraq might be regarded as an NRM. While Islam in general does not distinguish between the various parts of life - secular, political, or sacred - historically, orthodox Shiism has been politically "quietist," meaning that it does not directly engage in politics but focuses instead on religious life. In the more traditional sense also, Shiism does not openly advocate martyrdom, although there are historic examples of martyrs for the faith. These traditional viewpoints are upheld by Ayatollah Sistani. However, Shiism changed in the wake of the Khomeini revolution in Iran in 1979, which led to increasing assertiveness among certain groups of Shias in the Middle East. Muqtada al-Sadr's movement believes that Shias should be directly involved in the political life of Iraq and, moreover, should fight for control of the state.

Sadr's movement has its roots in the policies of Saddam Hussein, particularly those toward the Shias. In the 1990s, following Shia-driven criticism against the state, Saddam drained the Shia-inhabited marshes in the south, forcing perhaps a half million people off their land. These displaced Shias then settled in Baghdad's slums, where they became disciples of Sadr's father, Muhammad, an educated member of the clergy and a Grand Ayatollah. In January 1999, Saddam's secret police tried to pressure Muhammad Sadr to end his criticisms of the state, but he continued to speak out against Saddam's regime. As a result, he was killed the next month, along with two of his sons and their sister, leaving only the youngest, Muqtada.

Muqtada al-Sadr, fearing for his life, went into hiding, only to reemerge with the fall of Saddam in April 2003. He is, by the usual Shia criteria, an unqualified and unschooled cleric. Shias generally choose the most learned and experienced cleric as their leader, one who has passed through a long period of religious training; this status in not usually attained until a cleric is in the latter years of his life. Muqtada, by contrast, does not fit this description. In his case, his base of support comes largely from Shias who followed his father. Indeed, many of these followers have remained loyal to his father and still follow him despite his death. Thus they recognized his surviving son, Muqtada, as their leader primarily through his lineage to his father, a practice that is not uncommon historically in the religion.

Although the young "cleric" is not at all eminent by the usual criteria and does not command the respect of the majority of Shias in Iraq, he nevertheless is revered by his followers. He is charismatic, forceful in his language against the United States and its occupation of Iraq, and maintains the image of a tough guy who is willing to take on the world's remaining super power and the revered clerics at Najaf. However, his authority is questioned by the majority of Shia Muslims in Iraq and is not recognized by the four Ayatollahs in Najaf. In that sense, his movement is a NRM.

It was profoundly unwise for the United States to execute a warrant for the arrest of Muqtada in March 2004. When U.S. forces went after him, he retreated to a sacred shrine in Najaf, which the United States could not attack militarily because of the enormous outrage such an attack would have created among Muslims everywhere. By U.S. counts, American forces killed at least 1,500 Iraqis in the initial stages of the fight against Muqtada's fighters. Perhaps more damaging, the U.S. offensive in Najaf and Karbala angered and alienated Shias everywhere. There were demonstrations involving as many as 100,000 Shias in Lebanon. Even in Bahrain, a loyal U.S. ally, the Sultan felt he had to turn on the United States and disagree with their decision to go after the young cleric.

Sadr thus became a symbol of Shia opposition to the United States and its strong-arm military tactics. Moreover, the entire episode gave a powerful impetus to Shia political movements in Pakistan, Iran, Lebanon and elsewhere, not to mention in Iraq. The episode also increased the potential for the Sadr movement to strengthen links with Shia NRMs in other parts of the world. Thus, it is important to note that the movement appears to be larger than just the persona of its leader. It represents resistance to a perceived occupation by a foreign invader, and it would continue to exist if Sadr were killed.

Both before and after the Iraqi elections in January 2005, the question about the Sadr movement was which way it would go, either joining the political process or continuing to be a destabilizing force in Iraq. Its transition into parliamentary politics may be seen as more likely if it can be co-opted into the political decisionmaking process under the new government. Employment opportunities and improved health and sanitation facilities in Sadr City could go a long way in improving relations and the current state of affairs. The United States can facilitate this transition and bring an end to the current impasse.

It is important to observe that the Shias are not the only Islamic sect to produce NRMs. In Pakistan and Afghanistan, Sunni extremists are alive and well in areas where the remnants of Al-Qaeda and the Taliban have moved into tribal areas beyond government control. Similar to the Sadr movement, the Taliban has many characteristics that make it a NRM. In Pakistan, Sunni-inspired NRMs are bent on evicting Hindu India from all of Kashmir. The Taliban, Al-Qaeda, and other "Salafists" have given a different interpretation to certain passages in the Quran. For example, the Quran's reference to the merchants and others living in Mecca at the time when Muhammad fled that city for Medina, as "pagans" and "infidels" is now applicable to the Americans living in Saudi Arabia, who henceforth are targets to be attacked. This interpretation calls on Muslims everywhere to rise up and fight in defense of the faith. It is this worldview that most likely is influencing attacks such as the March 2004 Madrid bombings.

In terms of how the United States is perceived in the Middle East, it is largely impossible to decouple views of American policies and the threats these policies are seen to pose to the Muslim world from those of American society. However, Arabs and Muslims in this region, like most non-Americans, do make a distinction between "America" the idea, and the U.S. government and its policies. America the idea is appealing; cherished American values of freedom, individual liberty, and democracy are respected and applauded.[33]

But U.S. foreign policy in the Middle East, particularly its strong and unswerving support of Israel and its current war against terrorism and "Islam," have made the United States an object of hate. And this hatred is expressed in ways ranging from demonization and fatwahs to outright attacks on Americans. Moreover, U.S. support of authoritarian regimes such as Saudi Arabia and Egypt is juxtaposed against the rhetoric of freedom and democracy. Specific U.S. actions can be — and are likely to be — negatively linked or interpreted in terms of global actions that would otherwise be seen as benign. Thus, the United States is perceived as evil and out to destroy Islam; it therefore must be fought in order to defend the faith. By locating the "enemy" of Islam and subsuming their message under this framework, the Islamists have elevated their struggle, placing it in the cosmic realm.

CHRISTIANITY, ISLAM, AND THE POST-CHRISTIAN WEST

For scholar Jack Miles,[34] given the historical relations between Muslims and the Christian West, which for centuries have been characterized by quarrels, dissensions, and conflicts, it is no wonder that a deep chasm of mutual distrust continues to exist not just between followers of the two faiths but also between the Muslim *umma* and the secular West. In 1965, the bishops of the Catholic Church issued a bold statement pleading for both sides to "forget the past, and urging that a sincere effort be made to achieve mutual understanding. . . ."[32] Thirty-six years later when Pope John Paul II visited Syria in 2001, he went further in his call for rapprochement. "As members of one human family and as believers," he said, "we have obligations to the common good, to justice and to solidarity."[35] In the wake of September 11th, there were a number of calls for dialogue and understanding by leaders of both faiths in the United States. In spite of these efforts, however, deep suspicion and misunderstanding still prevail. In the words of one Christian theologian, "the large majority of Christians and Muslims continue to view each other with detailed ignorance."[36] Like it or not, the secular West — for powerful historical reasons — is heir to this estrangement.

Christianity and Islam today comprise well over 40 percent of the world's population, and Christian-Muslim relations have become a central concern in global politics. The ways in which these two communities of believers relate and understand each other will have profound consequences for the future. For Christians, the rapid growth of Islam in the West, particularly in France, England, and the United States, is a cause for grave concern. For Muslims, the current war on terrorism, perceived by them as "a war against Islam," is a wake up call for Muslims to defend their faith. For both communities, "detailed ignorance" remains a formidable barrier to meaningful dialogue and rapprochement.

Regarding the current crises in Islam, Miles' metaphor, one contested by other scholars of Islam, is a hijacked airplane. If the airplane is hijacked — as Islam arguably is by the radicals — then the right response is to talk to the passengers and persuade them to retake the plane. The United States should be in dialogue with Muslims throughout the world to aid in this process. A first step in this direction would be to engage and elicit the aid of educated Muslims such as Tariq Ramadan and others, as militants for peace.[37]

Moreover, the United States needs to develop a better "story," one that would enable it to speak of the Muslim world as Muslim and of the history behind current tensions between the United States and that world. The American story, continuing the European story, tells of an evolution of primary allegiance from religion to nation. Because world Islam has not evolved in the same way, American or other western actions undertaken for reasons of state may easily be interpreted as actions undertaken for reasons of religion. The needed story would place these two narratives in an intelligible and mutually acceptable relationship.

Miles notes a 1797 treaty with Tripoli, in which the United States declared that America was "in no sense founded on Christianity." But was the American national identity, thus announced, comprehensible to the Muslims who signed the treaty?

Miles' answer begins, essentially, in the fifth century with the fall of the Roman Empire in the West. At that point, clerical government — pope, bishops, priests, and monks — moved into the vacuum created by the collapse of civil government in Western Europe. In the East, the Roman (Byzantine) Empire continued and grew stronger during the sixth century. In the seventh, however, Islam replaced the Empire in all its originally Semitic territories plus Spain, and then began its great eastward expansion.

In 751, when the Arab armies defeated the Chinese on the banks of the Talas River near Lake Balkhash, Islamic expansion and influence into Central Asia took root. This eastward expansion continued with the capture of Delhi and the eventual Islamization of Northern India. Even during the series of Mongol conquests that came a few centuries later, Islam continued its eastward expansion. The campaigns of Timur the Lame were brutal; and according to one analyst, "this was the politics of force."[38] In 2003, when Saddam Hussein emphasized the idea of a terrible foreign threat to Baghdad before his own seizure by U.S. forces, "he referred not to earlier Christian attacks on Islam (including the British, who seized the city in both world wars) but to the Mongols. Indeed, when Baghdad fell in 1258, to a Mongol army under Hulegu, reputedly hundreds of thousands were slaughtered."[39] Yet from Sinkiang to the Caucasus, the Mongol conquerors adopted the religion of the conquered.

Islam owed its successes to inheritances from both Judaism and Christianity — from the former the notion of a supremely authoritative text (Torah/Quran) and from the latter the sense of a single world community under God (the universal or "catholic" church/the *umma* or "nation" of all believers). In their global ambition, Islam and Christianity were fraternal twins, the twin inheritors of the Roman Empire. However, Islam's cohesion, proselytizing zeal, and military power initially propelled it toward greater dominance. The Mediterranean became an "Islamic lake," and Western Europe was forced into defensive isolation.

Yet later Christianity began to expand as well, into Nordic and Slavic Europe and later, dramatically, into the Americas. Between 1500 and 1800, Christianity doubled in size. Meanwhile, Hindu resistance had halted the Islamic move eastward, just as the Christian resistance in Europe, symbolized by the re-conquest of Spain, began to reverse it in the north. When Britain replaced the Islamic moguls as rulers of India and Romanov Russia began its eastward march to the Pacific, the *umma* began to feel itself encircled.

A second and easily missed phase of this history began with the struggles within Christianity, whether between Catholics and Protestants, as on the continent, or between contending groups of Protestants, as in Britain. This was the process that eventually elevated national over religious allegiance in the West. The Peace of Augsburg in 1551 and the Treaty of Westphalia in 1648 ended truly religious warfare in Europe. The latter treaty, which ended the long, brutal Thirty Years War, laid the groundwork for secular international relations as we have known them. It ended not just the dominance of the Catholic Church in political affairs in Europe but also the dream of some that a reformed but equally universal church could replace it.

In place of that dream of universality was the great compromise of Westphalia: each national leader could be "pope" within his country but none could expand his "papacy" into another nation. The United States, a political creation of the post-Westphalian era, reflected precisely this combination of piety and reason at its foundation. Its constitution forbade a national religion but did not prevent the individual states from having their own (that was not definitively ended until the 14th Amendment in the mid-19th century).

In Europe, meanwhile, the fault-lines of allegiance and ideology ceased being religious and became national, as well as radical versus conservative. During the Enlightenment of the later 17th and 18th century, religion as a cultural force grew weaker in Europe, while nationalism grew stronger. Thus, Protestant Britain and Catholic Austria — both conservative monarchies — joined forces across sectarian lines to defeat radical France at Waterloo. Nationalism and the political agendas of ruling classes now trumped religion as never before. And it is in this context that the 1797 Tripoli treaty must be considered.

For the United States, the meaning of the "in no sense Christian" clause in the treaty was that "un-religion" was possible without irreligion or anti-religion. That is to say, all religions could be permitted while none would be "state sponsored."

But in all likelihood that set of notions was literally incomprehensible to America's Islamic interlocutors. Just as Pope Pius IX later would seek tolerance of Catholics in non-Catholic lands but was not prepared to grant non-believers the same rights in Catholic lands, so America's Islamic interlocutors in 1797 would have said that tolerance meant disobeying God. Remarkably and yet understandably, the Arabic translation of the treaty replaces the American declaration of religious neutrality between the two parties with a rambling set of considerations conducing against war on the North African side but without making any across-the-board statement about religion or religions.

During the two centuries that separate the Treaty of Tripoli from the current "war on terror," the *umma* has suffered one battlefield reverse after another at the hands of the West and its allies, culminating in the abolition of the caliphate in 1917 and the establishment of the State of Israel in 1947. Do most Muslims see these reverses as victories over various Muslim-majority nations by various Western nations along with world Jewry as a nation rather than a religion? Or, since Islam has had no religious wars comparable to those of the Christian West and no Peace of Westphalia signifying a movement from religious to national allegiance, are these victories seen rather as religiously Christian and religiously Jewish victories?

If the latter is often or even sometimes the case, then from a policy perspective, is it conceivable that the United States could now undertake a diplomatic initiative to present this country as "in no sense founded on Christianity"? This time it would need to go beyond the Treaty of Tripoli with a far more sophisticated and self-conscious explanation of what such a phrase means and does not mean and what it promises non-Christian nations that have diplomatic, cultural, and economic relations with the United States. Such an effort would encompass not only a reaching-out to Islam but also a real movement in unraveling the Israel-Palestinian conflict. As things stand, the secular approach of the United States and its industrial allies has fitted relatively comfortably with Asia's economic globalization, but China and India do not share with the West and the *umma* the Roman imperial heritage of global ambition in the name of God. The fact that Western secularism has eased Western relations with China and India has only increased Islam's sense that it is encircled and, indeed, under siege.

Surely, part of the answer is to address religion and religious freedom frontally, because no two nations with religious freedom have fought one another. That may mean that U.S. policy should give less pride of place to electoral democracy and more to religious freedom. There is some sense in which the clash with Islam is inevitable, so U.S. policy should try to blur the edges of that clash, not sharpen them. Apocalyptic visions feed on mirror images, so the more U.S. policy can be slow, boring and the like, the better.

If there is any resemblance between our current circumstances and those of the Cold War, this time we should not aspire to the military destruction of our opponent, even in the long run. Rather, we should bend every effort to keep the cold war from becoming hot. The Islamic world needs to understand and believe that the United States has no interest in imposing its will and its way of life on Islamic peoples, and above all that it has no interest in imposing the Christianity that the *umma* still so powerfully associates with the West. On the other hand, U.S. policymakers should try to adjust their mental map of relations with the Islamic world from one based on a historic sense of "conflict" to thinking of relationships along a continuum that encompasses a wide range of issues.

SCANNING FOR OTHER NRMS

Are there potential NRMs, even violent ones, apart from those spawned by Islamic radicalism? The Rashtriya Swayamsevak Sangh (RSS) in India, an ultra-Hindu nationalist movement, is one such organization. It has all the characteristics of a NRM. It espouses a strong and militant religious philosophy based on exclusivity and hate. After the assassination of Gandhi in 1948, the movement was banned for a few years by the Indian government because of its acts of violence and terrorism and its exhortation to followers to resort to terrorist methods in the promulgation of its religious ideas. In the 1990s, under the government led by the Bharatiya Janata Party (BJP), its role and influence in India grew and continues to grow even today. During the BJP's tenure in political office, the party was divided over associations with the RSS, with former Prime Minister Atal Bihari Vajpayee regarded as a soft-liner on Hindu nationalist issues and the party's president and deputy Prime Minister, L. K. Advani, as the hardliner. But the RSS continued to gain momentum and was engaged in violence, particularly against what it viewed to be threats against the Hindu state, namely Muslims and Christians. Their religious view, with its cosmic dimension, remains a threat to the idea of India as a secular state.

Several extremist religious Zionist groups in Israel are also NRMs, and they will continue to pose a threat to peace and stability in the Middle East. For many of them, the "holy land" goes beyond Palestine to Jordan and Syria, and this land, too, must be reclaimed for Judaism, by force if necessary.

The Lord's Resistance Army in Uganda may also be a dangerous NRM, although it is one that poses no threat to the United States. Nigeria is another potential problem. Islamic extremists in the Northern region of Kano are determined to institute Sharia law in spite of the fact that Nigeria is a secular state. The Hausa-Ibo war of the late 1960s could have been much worse and much more religious in character but for the restraint of General Yakubu Gowon. While continued religious conflicts between Muslims and Christians in Nigeria can undermine the integrity of the state, they do not pose that much of a threat to U.S. interests in the region except, perhaps, if these potential conflicts affect access to Nigeria's oil reserves in the North.

A much bigger question mark is China, where the growing sex imbalance means that there will be increasing numbers of unemployed males, breeding grounds for all sorts of discontent, including religiously based discontent. So far, the leading new religious groups have been Christian, and the predominant groups there have been easy-going. But in the western province of Xinjiang, tensions between Han

Chinese and the indigenous Muslim Uighurs continue to be a source of turmoil. The ongoing Uighur struggle to carve out Xinjiang as a Muslim state could have grave consequences not only for China but also for other bordering Central Asian states such as Kazakhstan. Even the Falun Gong, not very radical by most standards, might become more radical if it continues to be persecuted by the government. In looking for conditions that are fertile for NRMs, the role of demographics should be considered carefully. The population of India has the same age structure as that of China, so it too should be watched.

In Thailand and the Philippines, local grievances by Muslim populations have fused with more global Islamic visions. This kind of conflation is common, as global movements typically reinterpret global issues to relate locally, thus creating adherents to the global movement. This mixing of local and global is compounded by the Arabs in Indonesia, who have been returning to the madrassas in the Middle East, particularly in Yemen, and bringing back to the region radical interpretations of the Islamic faith.

Again, the class bases of NRMs and of their leadership are something to watch. In part, assumptions about the class basis of NRMs are artifacts of previous research. In the 1970s in the United States, for instance, the focus on white middle-class adherents obscured the more numerous Latino and black groups. However, different NRMs occupy different niches in different places. The RSS is largely middle class, as is the BJP. But Sadr's movement in Iraq has capitalized on the dispossessed, urban poor.

Finally, it is worth asking: Are NRMs really religious or political? This distinction is hard to parse, all the more so because it involves the other distinction of "local vs. global" (See Figure 1).

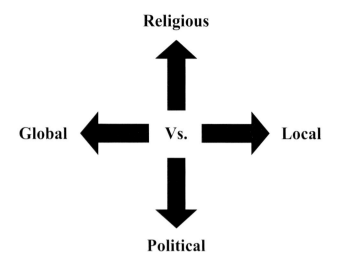

Figure 1. Key Movement Distinctions

The Irish Republican Army (IRA) in Northern Ireland, for instance, had political aims but those aims were circumscribed to that region; they were local. It also had a religious base, but that base was more ethnic than theological. So it might be defined as local, while straddling the political-religious distinction. Because it was local, it was one of few cases where money, in the form of British development assistance, seemed effective at both "drying the swamp" for new recruits and giving those who were aging out of terrorism a sense that they had other, legitimate alternatives for employment.

Al-Qaeda, as a NRM, however, is both global and religious in its aims. Statements from bin-Laden call for a worldwide uprising of Muslims, with the primary aim of defending the faith against what he sees as an imminent threat — the United States and apostate Muslim governments. Therefore, the movement has global ambitions and is engaging in violence for religious aims — the defense of the faith.

In most cases, the role of the state is key to understanding a crucial aspect of religious violence. If the state confronts a NRM and the latter perceives this as an attempt to undermine its existence, then that NRM is more likely to turn to violence. When NRMs speak of "self defense," they generally mean it. An excellent historical example of that is the Sikh religious movement, a NRM that was born with pacifist aims. However, after coming under attack from the Muslim Mughal Empire and following the execution of several of its key leaders at the hands of the monarchy, the movement formed a militant wing to defend the faith.

These examples suggest that if the government is close to the country's main religious group, then it will treat any apostate NRM as a criminal group and deal with it accordingly. By contrast, if the new group has deeper roots in national society, then the government will seek allies in controlling it. It is also worth considering that, in many respects, Islam today resembles Christianity three or four centuries ago. The Calvinists of that era had the certitude of cosmic warriors, yet they ultimately became the most enlightened of Christians. So, too, the Salafi movement, which began in the late 19th century, attempted to accommodate Islam to the requirements of global modernity by fashioning historically specific, metaphorical, or even purely apologetic understandings of the Quran. "This approach enabled them to justify in Islamic terms the adoption of European political, economic, and civic institutions, which they regarded as progressive and modern."[40] Thus, perhaps the watchword for policy should be trying to guide Islamic NRMs toward the social mainstream of the Muslim world, daunting though that task may appear at present.

5. CONCLUSION

The rise of religious movements in the late 20th century with a proclivity toward violence and terrorism — predominantly Islamic extremism — has significantly changed the landscape of international politics. It has also shifted the focus in analyzing the international system from the "power struggle" of Cold War politics and its attendant conceptual toolbox to a reality that emphasizes culture, violence in the name of religion, identity, and nationalism. Moreover, it has presented both a challenge and an opportunity for the intelligence community to understand the nuances of this new phenomenon and to help craft appropriate strategies to deal with this new threat to U.S. security and national interest.

This report has sought to provide both perspective and comparative angles of vision on that religious violence, as well as to identify new religious movements that might pose foreign policy challenges to the United States, if not real security threats. Most of the non-Islamic terrorist groups — the Basque separatists known as ETA, the IRA, the Tamil Tigers, the Identity Movement, the Solar Temple, and others — pale by comparison to Islamic terrorism in their effect on the landscape of international politics, even if they have some religious motivation. By contrast with all the others, the Islamic form of religiously motivated terrorism has a geographical base across many countries and a preexisting organizational network. Its ideology, rather than utterly new and therefore dependent on a charismatic leader, is the revival of something quite old with menacing variations.

Using the "cosmic war" concept as its overarching framework, this report explored the causes and motivations of religiously inspired violence and the roles played by both governments and New Religious Movements in using, facilitating, and mitigating this type of violence — and sometimes attempting all three in turn. Some impulses to violence do have their roots in religion.

Religious fundamentalists and extremists base their commitments on founding myths, decisive stories, inspiring narratives, and forthright commands found in their scriptures — all these are indicators to which intelligence can be attentive. It should be sensitive to the use of apocalyptic language by particular groups, especially in discussing weapons of mass destruction. It should look for the language of dream, repentance, or sudden change of fortune. In contrast, personal piety is not especially important as an indicator of cosmic war.

In all of these stories and narratives, there is a dark side, one that identifies the Enemy with evil powers that God has set out to vanquish. This cosmic struggle between the forces of Good and Evil, therefore, is the key to understanding how religiously inspired violence is perceived by its perpetrators and what motivates them to kill in the name of God. Thus, the transcendence of religion, with its impulse to engage in a war between Good versus Evil, provides a ready justification for the "extremists" to commit unspeakable acts of violence. That "evil" exists in the world is clearly not a contentious or wavering issue for the "warriors" of holy zeal. For them cosmic war is defensive, not offensive.

States find themselves in a difficult position when confronting cosmic war. Tactically, the more states turn to military instruments, the more they run the risk of validating the theology of the cosmic warriors. More strategically, states like Saudi Arabia that have sought to strike implicit bargains with religious extremists run great risk of losing control. That is particularly true because states have the most difficulty engaging cosmic warriors on what might be called the "spiritual-ideological" level. And this is due mainly to a deep lack of understanding of this phenomenon.

In assessing whether NRMs will turn to violence, two factors bear watching: the nature of an NRM's leadership, and the kind of response it confronts from society and the government. NRM leaders are often inexperienced and are prone to exaggerate external threats to retain the allegiance of their followers. Again, the more that governments seem to validate those leaders' apocalyptic visions, the greater the likelihood of mass suicide or other violence. Muqtada al-Sadr's movement in Iraq fits the definition of a NRM, and so the NRM framework is useful in assessing whether the threat of cosmic war he poses can be mitigated.

For the intelligence community, a different set of conceptual tools must be employed to better understand this new reality. It requires both understanding of religions and knowledge of non-Western culture and history as seen through a non-Western lens. For an analyst who is American by culture and training, this is a formidable task but one that is not insurmountable. The lens through which one views cosmic war and state response can be helpful. The next steps in building a framework for thinking about religion and conflict or violence might be to look in more depth at the particulars of religious extremists — such as their leadership or their patterns of education and indoctrination.

REFERENCES

Abrahamian, Ervand. *Iran Between Two Revolutions.* Princeton, NJ: Princeton University Press, 1982.

Almond, Gabriel, Scott Appleby and Emmanuel Sivan, *Strong Religion: The Rise of Fundamentalisms Around the World.* Chicago: The University of Chicago Press, 2003.

Armstrong, Karen and Susannah Heschel, "Fundamentalism and the Modern World," *Sojourners*, Vol. 31, No. 2, March-April 2002.

Black, Jeremy. "The Western Encounter with Islam," *Orbis*, Winter, 2004, p. 21.

Borelli, John. "Christian-Muslim Relations in the United States: Reflections for the Future After Two decades of Experience," *The Muslim World*, Vol. 94, July 2004, p. 321.

Brannan, David W. "The Evolution of the Church of Israel: Dangerous Mutations," *Terrorism and Political Violence,* Autumn 1999.

Brannan, David W. "A Response to Professor Kushner: Terrorism in America Reviewed," *Studies in Conflict and Terrorism,* October—November 2002.

Brannan, David W., et al. "Talking to Terrorists: Towards an Independent Analytical Framework for the Study of Violent Sub-State Activism, *Studies in Conflict and Terrorism,* January 2001.

Brown, Carl L. *Religion and State: The Muslim Approach to Politics.* New York: Columbia University Press, 2000.

Calvert, John. "The Islamist Syndrome of Cultural Confrontation," *Orbis*, Spring, 2002, p. 349.

Calvert, John. "The Mythic Foundations of Radical Islam," *Orbis*, Winter 2004, p. 34.

Cole, Juan. *Colonialism and Revolution in the Middle East: Social and Cultural Origins of Egypt's 'Urabi Movement.* Princeton, NJ: Princeton University Press, 1993.

Cole, Juan, ed. *Comparing Muslim Societies: Knowledge and the State in a World Civilization.* Ann Arbor, MI: University of Michigan Press, 1992.

Cole, Juan. *Roots of North Indian Shiism in Iran and Iraq: Religion and State in Awadh, 1722-1859.* Delhi: New York Oxford University Press, 1989.

Cole, Juan. *Sacred Space and Holy War: The Politics, Culture and History of Shi'ite Islam.* New York: I.B. Tauris, 2002.

Fox, Jonathan. "Religion and State Failure: An Examination of the Extent and Magnitude of Religious Conflict from 1950 to 1996," *International Political Science Review*, Vol. 25, No. 1, 2004, pp. 55 and 64.

Galtung, Johan. "Religions, Hard and Soft," *Cross Currents*, Vol. 47, Winter 1997-98, 437-50.

George, John, and Laird Wilcox. *American Extremists: Militias, Supremacists, Klansmen, Communists, & Others.* Amherst, NY: Prometheus Books, 1996.

Introvigne, Massimo. "'There Is No Place for Us to Go but Up': New Religious Movements and Violence," *Social Compass*, Vol. 49, No. 2, 2002, p. 220.

Jenkins, Philip. *Images of Terror: What We Can and Can't Know About Terrorism.* New York: Aldine de Gruyter, 2003.

Jenkins, Philip. *Mystics and Messiahs: Cults and New Religions in American History.* New York: Oxford University Press, 2000.

Jenkins, Philip. *The Next Christendom: The Coming of Global Christianity.* New York: Oxford University Press, 2002.

Juergensmeyer, Mark. *Global Religions: an Introduction.* New York: Oxford University Press, 2003.

Juergensmeyer, Mark. *The New Cold War? Religious Nationalism Confronts the Secular State.* Berkeley, CA: University of California Press, 1993.

Juergensmeyer, Mark. *Terror in the Mind of God: The Global Rise of Religious Violence* (3rd ed.), (Berkeley, CA: University of California Press, 2003).

Kimball, Charles. "Towards a More Hopeful Future: Obstacles and Opportunities in Christian-Muslim Relations," *The Muslim World*, Vol. 94, July 2004, p. 379.

Lofland, John. *Doomsday Cult.* New York: John Wiley & Sons, Inc., 1978.

Lofland, John. *Protest: Studies of Collective Behavior and Social Movements.* New York: Transaction Publishers, 1990.

Lofland. John and Rodney Stark, "Becoming a World-Saver," *American Sociological Review,* Vol. 30, 195, pp. 805-19.

Lustick, Ian. *Arabs in the Jewish State: Israel's Control of a National Minority.* Austin, TX: University of Texas Press, 1980.

Lustick, Ian. *For the Land and the Lord: Jewish Fundamentalism in Israel.* New York: Council on Foreign Relations, 1994.

Lustick, Ian. State Building Failure in British Ireland and French Algeria. Berkeley, CA: University of California Press, 1985.

Marty, Martin. "Is Religion the Problem," *Tikkun*, Vol. 17, No. 2, March-April 2002, pp. 19-21.

Melton, J. Gordon. "The Changing Scene of New Religious Movements: Observations from a Generation of Research," *Social Compass*, Vol. 42, No. 2, 1995, p.275.

Moghadam, Assaf. "Palestinian Suicide Terrorism in the Second Intifada: Motivations and Organizational Aspects," *Studies in Conflict and Terrorism*, Vol. 26, 2003, p. 72.

Origins: Catholic News Service Documentary Service, No. 31, 17 May 2001, p. 14.

Pro Diologo No. 107, 2001-02, p. 172.

Simon, Steven and Daniel Benjamin. *The Age of Sacred Terror: Radical Islam's War Against America*.New York: Random House, 2003.

Simon, Steven. *The New Terrorism and the Peace Process*. Ramat Gan: Bar-Ilan University 2002.

Simon, Steven, and Toby Dodge, ed. *Iraq at the Crossroads: State and Society in the Shadow of Regime Change*. Oxford: Oxford University Press, 2003.

Stark, Rodney. *The Future of Religion: Secularization, Revival and Cult Formation.* Berkeley: CA: University of California Press, 1985.

Stark, Rodney. *A Theory of Religion.* Rutgers, NJ: Rutgers University Press, 1996.

The 2002 Gallup Poll of the Islamic World. Princeton, NJ: Gallup, 2002.

White, Jonathan R. "Political Eschatology: A Theology of Antigovernment Extremism," *American Behavioral Scientist*, Vol. 44 No. 6, 6 February 2001, p. 939.

END NOTES

[1] Jonathan Fox, "Religion and State Failure: An Examination of the Extent and Magnitude of Religious Conflict from 1950 to 1996," *International Political Science Review*, Vol. 25, No. 1, 2004, pp. 55 and 64.

[2] *Ibid*, p. 55.

[3] Mark Juergensmeyer, *Terror in the Mind of God: The Global Rise of Religious Violence* (3rd ed.), (Berkeley, CA: University of California Press, 2003), p. 220.

[4] Examples of Juergensmeyer's research include: *Terror in the Mind of God: The Global Rise of Religious Violence* (New York: Oxford University Press, 2000); *The New Cold War? Religious Nationalism Confronts the Secular State* (Berkeley, CA: University of California Press, 1993); and *Global Religions: an Introduction* (New York: Oxford University Press, 2003).

[5] John Calvert, "The Islamist Syndrome of Cultural Confrontation," *Orbis*, Spring, 2002, p. 349.

[6] Johan Galtung, "Religions, Hard and Soft," *Cross Currents*, Vol. 47, Winter 1997-98, pp. 437-50

[7] Assaf Moghadam, "Palestinian Suicide Terrorism in the Second Intifada: Motivations and Organizational Aspects," *Studies in Conflict and Terrorism*, Vol. 26, 2003, p. 72.

[8] Examples of Juan Cole's research include: *Sacred Space and Holy War: The Politics, Culture and History of Shi'ite Islam* (New York: I.B. Tauris, 2002); *Colonialism and Revolution in the Middle East: Social and Cultural Origins of Egypt's 'Urabi Movement* (Princeton, NJ: Princeton University Press, 1993); *Roots of North Indian Shiism in Iran and Iraq: Religion and State in Awadh, 1722-1859* (Delhi: New York Oxford University Press, 1989); *Comparing Muslim Societies: Knowledge and the State in a World Civilization*, edited by Juan Cole (Ann Arbor, MI: University of Michigan Press, 1992).

[9] Jonathan R. White, "Political Eschatology: A Theology of Antigovernment Extremism," *American Behavioral Scientist*, Vol. 44 No. 6, 6 February 2001, p. 939.

[10] See Mark Juergensmeyer, The New Cold War (Berkeley, CA: University of California Press, 1993), p. 153.

[11] Mark Juergensmeyer, *Terror in the Mind of God*, 3rd Edition (Berkeley, CA: University of California Press, 2003), p. 234

[12] Examples of Steven Simon's research include: *The Age of Sacred Terror: Radical Islam's War Against America*, co-authored with Daniel Benjamin (New York: Random House, 2003); *Iraq at the Crossroads: State and Society in the Shadow of Regime Change*, edited by Toby Dodge and Steven Simon (Oxford: Oxford University Press, 2003); *The New Terrorism and the Peace Process* (Ramat Gan: Bar-Ilan University 2002).

[13] Examples of Ian Lustick's research include: *For the Land and the Lord: Jewish Fundamentalism in Israel* (New York: Council on Foreign Relations, 1994); *State Building Failure in British Ireland and French Algeria* (Berkeley, CA: University of California Press, 1985); *Arabs in the Jewish State: Israel's Control of a National Minority* (Austin, TX: University of Texas Press, 1980).

[14] Antonio Gramsci was a prolific writer. Most of his thoughts were expressed in the *Notebooks* written during his prison years between 1926 and 1936. Two of his pieces translated by Carl Marzani and Louis Marks are: *The Open Marxism of Antonio Gramsci* (New York: Cameron Associates, Inc., 1957), and *The Modern Prince and Other Writings by Antonio Gramsci* (London: Lawrence and Wishart, 1957). For Lustick's treatment of the distinction, see his *Unsettled States, Disputed Lands: Britain and Ireland, France and Algeria, Israel and the West Bank/Gaza* (Ithaca: Cornell University Press, 1993).

[15] Martin Marty, "Is Religion the Problem," *Tikkun*, Vol. 17, No. 2, March-April 2002, pp. 19-21.

[16] Gabriel Almond, Scott Appleby and Emmanuel Sivan, *Strong Religion: The Rise of Fundamentalisms Around the World* (Chicago, IL: The University of Chicago Press, 2003), p. 16.

[17] Gabriel Almond, et al, *Strong Religion: The Rise of Fundamentalisms Around the World* (Chicago, IL: The University of Chicago Press, 2003), p. 17.

[18] Karen Armstrong and Susannah Heschel, "Fundamentalism and the Modern World," *Sojourners*, Vol. 31, No. 2, March-April 2002, pp. 20-26.

[19] L Carl Brown, *Religion and State: The Muslim Approach to Politics* (New York: Columbia University Press, 2000), p. 169.

[20] Quoted in L. Carl Brown, *Religion and State: The Muslim Approach to Politics* (New York: Columbia University Press, 2000), p. 170.

[21] Quoted in L. Carl Brown, *Ibid*, p. 172.

[22] Ervand Abrahamian, *Iran Between Two Revolutions* (Princeton, NJ: Princeton University Press, 1982), p. 531.

[23] J. Gordon Melton, "The Changing Scene of New Religious Movements: Observations from a Generation of Research," *Social Compass*, Vol. 42, No. 2, 1995, p.275.

[24] Massimo Introvigne, "'There Is No Place for Us to Go but Up': New Religious Movements and Violence," *Social Compass*, Vol. 49, No. 2, 2002, p. 220.

[25] J. Gordon Melton, "The Changing Scene of New Religious Movements: Observations from a Generation of Research," *Ibid*, p. 274.

[26] Examples of John Lofland and Rodney Starks's research include: John Lofland, *Doomsday Cult* (New York: John Wiley & Sons, Inc., 1978), and *Protest: Studies of Collective Behavior and Social Movements* (New York: Transaction Publishers, 1990); Rodney Stark, *A Theory of Religion* (Rutgers, NJ: Rutgers University Press, 1996), and *The Future of Religion: Secularization, Revival and Cult Formation* (Berkeley: CA: University of California Press, 1985). Also, Lofland and Stark, "Becoming a World-Saver," *American Sociological Review,* Vol. 30, 195, pp. 805-19.

[27] Massimo Introvigne, "'There Is No Place for Us to Go but Up': New Religious Movements and Violence," *Ibid*, pp. 219-20.

[28] Massimo Introvigne, *Ibid*, p. 220.

[29] Jonathan R. White, "Political Eschatology: A Theology of Antigovernment Extremism," *Ibid*, p. 939.

[30] Jay E. Adams, *War Psalms of the Price of Peace,* (Philipsburg, NJ: Presbyterian and Reformed Publishing Company, 1991).

[31] Philip Jenkins, *The Next Christendom: The coming of Global Christianity* (Oxford; Oxford University Press, 2002).

[32] Kerry Nobel, *Tabernacle of Hate,* (Ontario Canada: Voyageur Publishing, 1998).

[33] As found in a 2002 Gallup Poll to the Muslim world. See: *The 2002 Gallup Poll of the Islamic World* (Princeton, NJ: Gallup, 2002).

[34] Quoted in John Borelli, "Christian-Muslim Relations in the United States: Reflections for the Future After Two decades of Experience," *The Muslim World*, Vol. 94, July 2004, p. 321.

[35] *Pro Diologo* No. 107, 2001-02, p. 172. Also published in *Origins: Catholic News Service Documentary Service*, No. 31, 17 May 2001, p. 14.

[36] Charles Kimball, "Towards a More Hopeful Future: Obstacles and Opportunities in Christian-Muslim Relations," *The Muslim World*, Vol. 94, July 2004, p. 379.

[37] Tariq Ramadan is the grandson of Hasan al-Bana, the founder of the Egyptian Brotherhood Movement, and currently a professor of religion and philosophy at a university in Switzerland. His is a moderate and well-respected voice in the Muslim community.

[38] Jeremy Black, "The Western Encounter with Islam," *Orbis*, Winter, 2004, p. 21.

---

[39] Quoted in Jeremy Black, "The Western Encounter with Islam," *Ibid*, p. 21.

[40] John Calvert, "The Mythic Foundations of Radical Islam," *Orbis*, Winter 2004, p. 34.